Karl Shaw is a freelan
He lives with his wife and two sons in Stoke-on-Trent, Staffordshire, and is the author of *Gross* and *The World Encyclopedia of Lies and Utter Fibs*.

GROSS 2

This Time It's Personal

Another Compendium of the Unspeakable,
Unpalatable, Unjust and Appalling

Karl Shaw

First published in Great Britain in 1994 by
Virgin Books
an imprint of Virgin Publishing Ltd
332 Ladbroke Grove
London W10 5AH

A catalogue record for this book is available from the
British Library

ISBN 0 86369 896 4

Typeset by Galleon Typesetting, Ipswich, Suffolk
Printed and bound in Great Britain by
Cox & Wyman Ltd, Reading, Berks

For Robert and Charlie.
Sorry boys, we needed the
money

Outside of a dog, a book
is a man's best friend.
Inside of a dog,
it's too dark to read
                    Groucho Marx

Contents

Entrée

During World War II, the British Minister of Food, Lord Woolton, carefully considered but finally rejected a plan proposed by his government scientists to feed the country on black pudding from left-over donations of human blood.

According to royal etiquette, any man infected with ringworm is not required to remove his hat in the presence of a British monarch.

In the Indian state of Baroda in the nineteenth century, the Maharajah had criminals executed by forcing elephants to stand on the unfortunates' heads.

When D. H. Lawrence died, his lover Frieda had his ashes tipped into a concrete mixer and incorporated into her brand new mantelpiece.

The Sour Toe Cocktail is an acquired taste exclusive to the Yukon Territory in Canada. The main ingredient is an amputated human toe which can be dunked in the spirit of your choice. The only hard and fast rule is,

'You can drink it fast, you can drink it slow, but the lips have got to touch the toe.' The drink was first created in 1973 by a Mountie who discovered an amputated human toe in an empty log cabin. The original artefact was used over 700 times before it was inadvertently swallowed by a miner.

No really, you shouldn't have . . .

Pope Pius IX sent Queen Isabel II of Spain a gift of the embalmed body of Saint Felix on the occasion of her birthday. She had it permanently displayed in a glass coffin in the Spanish royal chapel.

Every English monarch, from Henry I in 1135 until at least the beginning of the nineteenth century, has had two separate funeral ceremonies: one for their corpse, and another for the burial of their eviscerated entrails.

Some Malaysians eat the brains of live monkeys as an aphrodisiac. The monkey suffers slow torture as a bowl is fitted to its head above the ears, and its body is crammed into a tight box to prevent it from moving. The scalp is then cut open and the exposed brain eaten with a spoon or sucked out with a straw.

Maori tribesmen often preserved the elaborately tat-tooed heads of their deceased relatives to keep alive their memory. The heads would be steamed several times in an oven, smoked dry, and the hair carefully combed into a top-knot. In 1770 the British explorer

Sir Joseph Banks acquired the first specimen Maori head ever seen in Europe, and the heads suddenly became fashionably collectable. The Maoris quickly overcame their early objections to selling off the heads of their loved ones when they discovered that British museums and private collectors were prepared to pay generously for good quality, highly decorated specimens. As heads became scarce, unscrupulous Maori dealers would supply the untattooed heads of recently deceased slaves – few Europeans could tell the difference between a genuine relic and the head of a recently dead slave which had been freshly tattooed *post mortem*. By this time the greedy dealers were only one short step away from depriving living Maoris of their heads. In 1832 the gruesome practice had reached such horrific proportions that the head trade was finally made illegal.

Excluding rodent hair and bug excrement, the ten least appetising foreign bodies reported to have been found in a British loaf are: a human toenail (Humberside, 1989); a whole mouse (Preston, 1980); a toupee (Humberside, 1975); surgical support hose (Glasgow, 1977); a glass eye (Bristol, 1972): a rat's tail (Stoke-on-Trent, 1887); rat excrement (East Staffordshire, 1976); half an adult rat (Plymouth, 1988); 3 inches of soiled bandage (Tayside, 1986); and a condom (West Midlands, 1988).

In a single day in December 1938, Joseph Stalin signed 3,182 death warrants.

Professional chariot racers in Ancient Rome used to build up their muscles by drinking dried boar's dung in water.

During China's cultural revolution in the sixties and seventies, members of Mao Tse-tung's Red Guard ate the flesh of their enemies to show their leader that they were fully class-conscious.

The uncertainties of medical science in the Middle Ages regularly produced premature burials – embarrassing for the undertaker and a pain in the arse for the victim – and so it became normal to observe a three-day waiting period before the funeral took place, just to be on the safe side. It was not unknown for corpses to revive themselves within three days but, as a Canterbury monk observed, recoveries after more than a week were more unusual. Anyone lucky enough to survive Extreme Unction, however, soon discovered that life for an ex-corpse wasn't all bier and skittles: there were certain strings attached. People who carried on living after receiving the last rites were not allowed to eat meat, to walk barefoot, or to have sex.

Avocado was the Aztec word for testicle – the fruit reminded them of a scrotum.

When the mistress of the nineteenth-century French novelist 'Eugene' Sue died, she willed him her skin with instructions that he should bind a book with it. He did.

The African Bafum-Bansaw tribe gave their victims an enema before they ate them by forcing boiling palm oil into their bowels. Apparently it made the flesh more tender.

King Edward VII owned a golf bag made from an elephant's penis. It was a birthday present given to him by an Indian Maharajah who had heard of the King's fondness for golf, big game hunting and adultery, but not necessarily in that order.

Fat corpses decompose more quickly than thin ones. The extra flab retains body heat, speeding the bacterial action which breaks down human tissue.

When General Kitchener was fighting the Boers in South Africa in 1900 he complained bitterly that the enemy didn't fight fairly. Apparently the bounders were always on the move or taking advantage of the surrounding cover, instead of standing quite still in the open to be shot down by British rifles and machine guns.

Although London's tap water is good enough for just under seven million of her subjects, the Queen never cleans her teeth in it, let alone drinks it.

Dried bulls' penises are sold as dog chews.

Bottoms up . . .

When Nelson died, his corpse was shipped home in a keg of brandy to preserve it. Although the Admiral's dead body had been bubbling away in it for days, it didn't stop his sailors from drinking the spirits later.

When Thomas à Becket's head was bashed in and the contents of his skull spilled out over the floor of Canterbury Cathedral in 1170, bystanders dipped pieces of cloth into his brains and saved them as holy relics.

During the Indian Mutiny of 1858, the British troops in India would strap captured mutineers across the muzzle of their loaded cannon and blast them to pieces. It was widely believed on both sides that the Almighty wouldn't be able to reassemble the bits of the body, and so the victim would be deprived of an afterlife. For many of the British officers stationed in India, butchering the natives ranked up there with pig-sticking as top sporting interludes in an otherwise tedious existence. One officer, H. H. Stansfield wrote home: 'It is very dull here, now and then a sepoy hanged or blown away, a cricket match or two, and a little quail shooting.'

In much the same way that chewing tobacco was used by Europeans and Americans, Fijian cannibals acquired a taste for hanks of salted human flesh.

British diners in America should beware of employing the phrase 'basket lunch': in the US it is an invitation to practise spontaneous fellatio.

Waiting for a grill like you

In Wisconsin, USA in 1989, John Weber was convicted for the murder of a seventeen-year-old schoolgirl, Carla Lenz. During the trial he confessed that he'd made pâté from his victim's leg and eaten it.

Eunuchs, traditionally employed to guard harems, were generally prisoners of war or slaves who were castrated, usually before puberty. The practice of castrating slaves for the eunuch trade was a risky business with a very high mortality rate. Although most of the time genitals were removed by a single razor cut, there were various other techniques of eunuch-making which involved crushing, striking and pulling actions. There were three different classifications of eunuch: Castrati, who had both penis and testicles cut off; Spadones, who had their testicles pulled off, and Thlibiae, who had their testicles rendered useless by crushing or bruising. There were also variations in procedures for the control of haemorrhage. As hot desert sand was considered the most efficient embrocation, the newly castrated were often buried up to their necks until the wound had healed.

netimes the wound would be cauterised with boiling oil and the patient planted in a fresh dung-hill. Very few boys survived the trauma, the agonising pain, the haemorrhage, and the subsequent burial in the arid heat, but it increased the market value of those who did. Many eunuchs had a silver quill hidden in their turbans, which they would insert into the urethra when they needed to urinate.

On 10 December 1898, the Empress Elizabeth, wife of Austria's Emperor Franz Josef, was assassinated on a quayside in Geneva by a 26-year-old Italian builder's labourer, Luigi Lenchini, who stabbed her through the heart. Lenchini later explained that he had nothing whatsoever against the Empress; he really wanted to kill King Umberto of Italy, but couldn't afford the extra 50 lire he needed to travel to Rome.

Donner kebab

One item of American folklore as yet untouched by Hollywood occurred in 1846 when 87 men, women and children set out on a 2000-mile trek to California, led by the Illinois farmer George Donner and his family. It was badly planned: they realised too late that they had set out at completely the wrong time of year, and the only way they could survive the winter was by eating each other. Of the original party, only 47 made it to the end of the trail. The decision to resort to cannibalism under such dire circumstances might have been excused as a grisly but understandable tale of a man chewing what he had to chew, had not some of the survivors struck a less than penitent attitude later. One, Lewis Keseberg, cheerfully admitted a preference for both human liver and brain soup. He paid an emotional tribute to George Donner's wife Tamsen, declaring, 'She was the healthiest woman I ever ate.' Later Keseberg found wealth when he opened a steakhouse.

Samuel Pepys chronicled his daily life in the minutest of detail, but in the nine years he kept his diary, only once does he mention his wife having a bath.

In the late 1960s, Mao Tse-tung confessed to his aides that he was secretly hoping that the USA would drop a nuclear bomb on a remote province of China and kill between ten and twenty million Chinese people: this would show the rest of the world, Mao explained, just how crazy the Americans really were.

A Private Function

The US actress Tallulah Bankhead once found herself in a cubicle in a ladies' lavatory without any toilet paper. She called out to the next cubicle, 'Darling, is there any tissue in there?'

The reply came: 'Sorry, no.'

'Any Kleenex?'

'Afraid not.'

'My dear,' continued Tallulah, 'can you change two fives for a ten?'

Jonathan Swift, author of *Gulliver's Travels*, wrote a treatise on excrement in 1733 called *Human Ordure* under the pen-name 'Dr Shit'.

It was once common for German farmers to stack piles of excrement – animal and human – in front of their farms and dwellings. The size of the pile was a way of showing off to your neighbours that you had loads of livestock and could afford a huge family.

The expression 'flying pasty', coined towards the end of the eighteenth century but now in disuse, described the antisocial act of wrapping excrement in paper and throwing it over a neighbour's wall.

The most reliable indicator of a nation's economy is the quality of the toilet paper it uses: thus argues the Croatian author Slavenka Drakulic in her book *How We Survived Communism and Even Laughed*. In Russia most toilet paper is like cardboard, whilst the Chinese still use newspaper. In 1993, the Yugoslavian newspaper *Politika* advised readers to use 100-dinar notes as 'each sheet of the real thing costs twice as much.' In Siberia, where no one can afford paper of any description, they use snow.

French soldiers at the battle of Crécy in 1346 nick-named the English 'the bare-bottomed army' because they were riddled with dysentery.

The daily bowel movements of the eighteenth-century King Ferdinand I of Naples were an utterly serious business: he always insisted on having a crowd of people around to keep him entertained while he strained. His father-in-law, the Austrian Emperor Joseph, was one of many who became privy to these unusual audiences, and noted later, 'We made conversation for more than half an hour, and I believe he would still be there if a terrible stench had not convinced us that all was over.' Ferdinand evidently also offered to show his father-in-law the fruits of his labours for closer inspection.

Soft soap

Apart from wine-making, there are very few uses that human bodily waste hasn't been put to by your ancestors. Stale urine and excrement, which both contain ammonia, were commonly used for bathing, and for washing clothing and linen right up until World War II. The urine used on wash day went by different names according to locality: in Lancashire it was called 'lant', and every yard had a communal 'lant-pot' for collecting it. In Yorkshire it was called 'weetin' or 'old waish'. Poor people bathed themselves in urine, and more often than not it wasn't even their own: streets and groups of houses in the 1840s frequently collected their urine in a common barrel. The custom continued in poorer working class areas for at least another 50 years. Cakes of animal excrement, added to cold water, also had a cleansing effect and were used instead of, or as an addition to, urine: Welsh peasants were fond of using pig manure as a popular alternative to soap. Women became so immune to the stench of stale urine and shit on wash days that when soap became popular they often complained that the suds made them nauseous. Dung never became quite as popular as urine, partly because people suspected

12

that it caused something known as 'the itch', but mostly because it had so many other uses, as a fertiliser, as a fuel or as a building material. For centuries most poor people used cow or horse dung as fuel; although the smell was incredibly offensive, it was free, easy to collect, simple to burn and gave out a great deal of heat. When coal became more easily available in the late eighteenth and early nineteenth centuries dung fuel became less common, but the practice continued in Cornwall. In the Aran Islands off the west coast of Ireland it was still the main source of heat in the 1930s.

Before flush toilets were invented most ordinary people used chamber pots, while royalty and the upper classes favoured the close-stool – an armchair with a strategically placed hole or a simple box with a hinged lid. Country people did it in the fields, and townies did it wherever they could.

In some parts of the world animal manure is sculpted into fashion jewellery. Visitors to the 1994 Winter Olympics in Norway were sold souvenir elk droppings at £7 a pair: these were dried, cooked in microwave ovens, painted with lacquer and worn as earrings.

The ultimate in lavatory books was published by Bourne, Jackson & Latimer in 1870, entitled *Stray Leaves From Japanese Papers*. The bound volume contained nothing but 400 blank leaves of toilet paper,

'A perfectly pure article for the toilet and lavatory, and a preventative for piles . . . confidently recommended as the best article ever produced for the particular purpose for which it was intended , . . soft, yet so strong as to bear a tight twist.'

In pre-public convenience Britain, London's parks were notorious for their desperate defecators. When Casanova travelled through St James's Park he noted with disgust, 'Six or seven people shitting in the bushes with their hinder parts turned towards the public.'

In Ancient Rome, rooms were rarely set aside for individual toilets. When a Roman needed to relieve himself he would summon a slave to bring a chamber pot and would do it there and then, irrespective of where he was or who was with him. By the first century, Rome had public latrines, but defecation continued to be a very communal affair. The Romans wiped their backsides with brine-soaked sponges on sticks, which were then rinsed out and left for the next user.

When the Dutch scholar Erasmus visited England in the sixteenth century, he described how the floors of the typical upper-class English home would be covered with a twenty-year-old crust of 'filth, spillings of beer, the remains of fish, spittle and vomit, excrement and urine of dogs and men, and other filthiness not to be named.'

Marketing techniques for toilet paper in the 1930s had little to do with quilts or labrador puppies: this was a war waged over the terrors of 'hard' and 'soft' brands. A typical US newspaper advertisement for 'soft' paper confidently asserted that hard paper was a major cause of what was referred to as 'rectal trouble'. An advertisement promoting Scot Tissue – 'the paper that doctors recommend' – informed the public that '65 per cent of all men and women in middle age suffer from troubles caused by inferior toilet paper.'

When Peter the Great's son, Alexis, went to Dresden in 1712 to marry a German Princess, the Elector of Hanover, Ernst August, noted with distaste in a letter to his wife that the Tsarevitch shat in his bedroom and wiped his backside with the curtains.

The 1883 publication *The Family Physician* blamed poor toilet design as a major cause of constipation in ladies. The ideal surroundings required to get the bowels moving freely, the late Victorians were urged, comprised 'a bright cheerful little chamber, where you might pass five or ten minutes with a certain amount of comfort, and moralise on things in general.'

In the very politest of French society, shit is only ever referred to as *les cinq lettres*.

The ancient ritual of inspecting one's faeces in the belief that the consistency and colour of your turds can reveal more about the state of your health than your GP ever could is still widely observed in Germany. This fixation with fibrous floaters has led to the evolution of a unique German flat-pan toilet design. The toilet bowl is built so that the faeces, instead of being deposited at the bottom, out of sight and out of mind, sit pertly in the middle of a shallow ceramic ledge, inviting inspection. Unfortunately, these turds tend to hang around on their little ledge even after a couple of brisk flushes, and instead of whirling off down the drain when they are supposed to, they have to be coaxed off with a stiff toilet brush.

When the first toilet paper was manufactured in the 1850s, it quickly became an unmentionable item, euphemistically advertised as 'curl papers' for hairdressing. By the 1870s, American ladies were carrying a personal supply of toilet paper hidden inside a fan. Britain's first soft toilet paper, which appeared in 1942, was available exclusively from Harrods.

In France, where the toilet paper is said to be of better quality than their banknotes, people are believed to be fussier about the quality of their toilet paper than anyone else in the world − well, almost. In order

to pass domestic sanitary regulations, British toilet
paper has to be edible.

Sherborne Lane in the City of London, was originally
called Shitteborwelane, because it was the site of a
particularly foul-smelling public latrine.

Britain spends about £70 million per annum on laxa-
tives – more per capita than any other country in
Europe.

For several centuries in Britain, the discovery of a
steaming turd in a public place would provoke the
popular, but now disued exclamation, 'Sirreverence!'.

Contrary to schoolyard myth, Thomas Crapper did
not invent the WC. That distinction belongs to Sir
John Harrington, godson and privy-maker to Queen
Elizabeth I, who had one of his very first prototype
flush toilets, complete with cistern, pan, overflow,
valve and waste pipe installed in her palace at
Richmond. Sadly, and in spite of the royal patronage,
his idea didn't catch on for another 200 years, and the
expression 'going for a Harring' never entered the
English language. Thomas Crapper did, however,

produce something called the Valveless Water Waste Preventer, the forerunner of the modern flush toilet system, which allowed water to flush the bowl only when required.

Samuel Pepys once noted in his diary that because his maid had forgotten to leave a chamber pot in his bedroom he had been forced to 'shit twice in the chimney fireplace'.

Some Like It Hot

In 1885 the US army captain and part-time naturalist and author John Bourke published a detailed description of the Urine Dance of the Zuni Indians of New Mexico. Bourke explained how he had been privileged to witness this unique ritual, which involved a dozen Zuni Indians dancing around a fire while eagerly drinking several gallons of fresh urine. When his hosts invited him to be their guest at a similar ceremonial dance, this time involving excrement, the captain made his excuses and left.

Louis XIV had a habit of granting audiences to people while he was sitting on his close-stool: some visitors, including the English ambassador Lord Portland, even regarded it as a special honour to be received by the Sun King in this manner. Louis in fact announced his betrothal to his second wife Madame de Maintenon whilst in the middle of a crap.

Rats can tread water for three days and can easily swim up waste pipes and enter homes through the S-bends of toilet systems. In the 1980s, a company from Omaha, USA patented a 'plastic rodent stopper' to be fitted in toilet bowls, after dozens of people reported that they had been bitten on the backside by rats while sitting on the toilet.

Although seventeenth-century France was considered to be the very pinnacle of high culture, it left a different impression on the Austrian-born Duchess of Orléans when she became the second wife of Louis XIV's brother. She wrote home of Paris in 1694: 'The multitude of people who shit in the street produces a smell so detestable that it cannot be endured.' She went on, 'There is one thing at court that I shall never get used to . . . the people stationed in the galleries in front of our rooms piss into all the corners. It is impossible to leave one's apartment without seeing someone pissing.'

Maybe it's because the modern flush toilet system was a British invention, or perhaps it's just because the English language has more words in it than any other, but of all the countries in Europe, Britain has developed the greatest proliferation of lavatorial euphemisms. The favourite of the sixteenth century was 'Jakes'; in the seventeenth century, it was 'closet', 'latrine' or 'necessary house'; in the eighteenth century 'bog' grew in popularity, along with 'water closet', 'the house of office', 'the little house', or the

colourful 'cackatorium'. 'Dunny' was also originally an
eighteenth-century British expression, which migrated
to Australia with a few thousands convicts and took a
firm hold down under. It now ranks at the top of the
Antipodean loo lexicon ahead of 'diddy', 'toot' and
'brasco'. Victorian Britons referred to the 'bog house',
the 'WC' and the 'toilet', from the French toilette. The
whole world has since borrowed the English term
'WC'. By and large, the French are happy to call
them *pissoirs*, or occasionally *Rambeteau*, after a
famous French prefect, or *Vespasienne*, a reference to
the Emperor who established Rome's first public
conveniences. Germany meanwhile has *Abort* (away
place), *stilles Örtchen* (silent little place), *Abtritt* (walk
away), *'D' und 'H'* (*Damen* and *Herren*), *Donnerbalken*
(thunder board), and the very silly *Plumsklo* (plop
closet). A Russian will usually ask for the *ubornaya*
(adornment place), a desperate Dutchman will require
the *bestekamer* (best room), while an Italian will
confusingly seek the *bagno* (bath) or sometimes the
gabinetto, a derivation of the French for cabinet room.

Royal Flush
Everywhere the Queen goes, her personal lavatory
seat cover made of white kid goes with her.

Whenever the Queen uses the lavatory a lady-in-
waiting guards the door to prevent anyone else from
using the convenience.

Queen Victoria was preoccupied with her bowels. She would summon her court doctor for a discussion on the subject up to six times a day. Even while she was away on her honeymoon, her physician received a surprise note from her one day, informing him: 'The bowels are acting fully.'

In his reckless youth, Prince Charles collected toilet seats.

The Queen's favourite royal anecdote tells of an occasion when she shared a horse-drawn carriage with a visiting (unnamed) African president. During their trip, one of the Queen's horses broke wind so loudly and forcibly that it couldn't be ignored, and so the Queen apologised to her guest. The African president whispered back, 'That's quite all right Ma'am . . . I thought it was the horse.'

Royals From Hell

The Russian Czar Paul, who was mad, snub-nosed and bald, once had a soldier scourged to death for referring to his Imperial Highness as 'baldy'. The Czar later issued a proclamation that the words 'baldy' and 'snub-nose' were henceforth banned and that anyone heard using them in the future would receive a similar treatment.

King Miguel of Portugal liked to toss live piglets in the air so he could catch them on the point of his sword.

Queen Victoria's father Edward, the Duke of Kent, was sacked as Governor of Gibraltar for flogging the garrison into a state of mutiny. He was known as 'the beast' because of his sadistic treatment of soldiers, and was so excited by the sight of men being whipped that he would wet his trousers.

Queen Henrietta, wife of the Belgian King Leopold II, kept a pet llama which she taught to spit in the face of anyone who stroked it.

Serbia's Prince George, eldest son and heir of King Peter I, was removed from the line of succession in 1909 after kicking his valet to death.

Portugal's King John V found a unique way of reconciling his two greatest – but on the face of it mutually exclusive – interests, namely prayer and sex: he copulated with nuns. The King had long-standing and quite open sexual relationships with the Sisters of the Odivelas Convent which resulted in at least three illegitimate sons.

The eighteenth-century Prussian King Frederick William I was considered by his contemporaries to have been extremely eccentric, not because he was a demented, vicious psychopath who would fly into uncontrollable rages and thrash the living daylights out of anyone who crossed him, and who once had to be restrained from murdering his own son, but because he washed his hands regularly.

Romania's deranged King Carol II was a sex-mad autocrat whose personal harem and tacky private life were the talk of Europe. He abolished all political parties and declared himself Royal Dictator, and had some of Bucharest's finest buildings demolished so that the sights of his machine guns had a clear view of the approaches to his home. He also insisted on personally picking Romania's football team for the 1930 World Cup Finals, where they beat Peru 3–1 but failed to reach the semi-finals, going out to the hosts and eventual winners, Uruguay. History will therefore remember King Carol II as a dangerous, sex-mad despot whose record in competitive international football was much better than Graham Taylor's.

George V once killed 39 tigers in one day. The Indian Maharajah Jay Singh of Alwar, although a notorious paedophile, was a personal friend of his and was the king's guest at Buckingham Palace in 1931. The Maharajah was also a keen big game hunter: he used live babies and elderly widows as tiger bait.

Emperor Menelik II of Ethiopia heard about America's exciting new means of executing criminals, the electric chair, and decided to order three. When they arrived, the Emperor found there was just one snag: a working electric chair required one thing that Ethiopia didn't have – electricity. He had one chair converted into a new throne and sent the other two back.

When England's 'mad' King George III first showed signs of mental illness, it was hushed up by his courtiers, who rallied around him by pretending to be mad themselves. The cat was finally let out of the bag in 1811 when he began his address to the House of Commons, 'My Lords and Peacocks . . .'

The certifiably insane Rajah of Akalkot reigned over the Indian state of Porbandor in the mid-nineteenth century. His problem was brought to the attention of the ruling British one day when, on a whim, he lopped off the ears and nose of a courtier.

Everywhere he went, Germany's Kaiser Wilhelm II carried with him a collection of photographs of all his dead Hohenzollern relatives dressed in their funeral attire.

Spain's Queen Maria Christina threw lavish fancy dress balls and encouraged her guests to dance and make merry until the early hours, but afterwards always sent them an itemised bill for the food and drink they had consumed.

The mad French King Charles VI became convinced that his legs and buttocks were made of glass and refused to travel by coach in case they shattered. He eventually became so unstable that his wife Queen Isabeau decided that it was too risky to share a bed with him, and ordered one of her servants, Odette de Champdivers, to wear her clothing and take her place. The King slept with Odette regularly, never once noticing the difference.

The Haitian King Henry Christophe ordered his personal bodyguards to prove their loyalty to him by marching over the edge of a 200-foot cliff to certain death. Those who disobeyed were tortured and executed. When the mad king's subjects finally rebelled against him in 1820, he cheated a lynch mob by shooting out his own brains.

The Turkish Sultan Murad IV beheaded anyone who annoyed him, no matter how trivial the offence, and daily enjoyed target-practice with his larquebus (a seventeenth-century long-barrelled gun) with innocent passers-by who strayed too close to the palace walls. He once stumbled across a party of women in a meadow and had them drowned because they were making too much noise.

Kaiser Wilhelm II had numerous diamond and sapphire rings, which he always wore with the stones facing inwards so that his handshake hurt people.

The French Empress Eugénie, wife of Napoleon III, attempted suicide by breaking the heads off phosphorus matches and drinking them dissolved in milk.

One day in 1933, the polo-playing Indian Maharajah Jay Singh Alwar had a bad game and decided to blame his horse, which had stumbled and thrown him. As an audience of British VIPs watched, the Maharajah poured a can of petrol over the polo pony and set fire to it.

Apart from being a professional drunken psychopath, Peter the Great was also a keen amateur surgeon and anatomist. Once on a trip to Holland, and just after a heavy meal, the Czar witnessed with fascination the anatomical dissection of a human cadaver. When two of his nauseous attendants made it clear that they didn't quite share his enthusiasm for the sight of the inner workings of the body laid bare, Peter forced them to bite into the muscles of the corpse. Although the Czar was not a particularly competent surgeon, no one dared to turn him down when he volunteered to wield the knife. When the Czarina Martha Apraxina, widow of his half-brother Theodore III, died of indigestion, Peter personally opened up her corpse just to find out if the rumour that she was still a virgin at the age of 49 was true. The Czar also once removed twenty pounds of water from the dropsical wife of a rich Russian merchant named Borst. Peter was extremely proud of his handiwork, but was furious when the woman selfishly died shortly afterwards. He ordered an autopsy to prove that he hadn't been responsible for the death. Unsurprisingly, the inquest found that Peter was entirely blameless.

When Persia's ruling monarch Reza Shah had an overnight stay in a remote village, all of the dogs within a one-mile radius were put down in case they barked and disturbed his sleep.

Sweden's seventeenth-century Queen Christina was mentally unbalanced and suffered from an irrational fear of fleas. She had a miniature four-inch cannon built which worked perfectly and spent most of her time firing tiny cannonballs at the fleas in her bedroom.

Turkey's Sultan Abdul Aziz developed a 'thing' about black ink and ordered every government document in existence to be rewritten in red. The order only took about twenty years to complete.

Denmark's King Christian VII was completely insane, but this didn't prevent him from being awarded honorary degrees by both Oxford and Cambridge Universities.

Frederick the Great, although renowned for his military genius, had a cruel disregard for human life. Wounded men were expected to find their own way off the battlefield and to hospital as best they could; neither were they given any rations. As only one in five who entered a Prussian military hospital came out alive, men deserted by the thousand rather than risk it, and hundreds more committed suicide. When campaign funds ran short Frederick saved money by skimping on his soldier's uniforms: there was so little fabric in them they couldn't even be fastened, and so many of his men froze to death.

When Sultan Abdul Aziz discovered that one of his servants shared his second name, he passed a law which made it illegal for anyone else to be named 'Aziz'. This was roughly comparable to banning the name 'Smith' in England.

Peter the Great's pride and joy was his Museum of Curiosities created to satisfy his perverse interest in freaks of nature. The items he collected included a man without genitals, a child with two heads, a five-footed sheep, a deformed foetus, the organs of a hermaphrodite, 'the hand of a man who died by excessive drinking with all its blood stagnated in the veins' and the corpses of Siamese twins. All these things became specimens in Peter's museum, individually pickled in huge alcohol-filled jars. The museum caretaker, a badly deformed dwarf, must have suspected that one day he too would be stuffed and put on display. One of Peter's prize curiosities was a pickled phallus, donated by the Prussian King Frederick William: it had caught Peter's eye on his trip to Berlin and the Prussian King was only too delighted to get rid of it. Peter thought it would be a good jape to persuade his wife Catherine to kiss it: she accepted his invitation, but only after he made it more attractive by offering to cut off her head if she declined.

When Egypt's King Menephta defeated the Libyans in 1300 BC he took home with him the penises of all his slain enemies as battle trophies.

Towards the end of the Ottoman Empire, Turkey's Sultans threw themselves into a belated effort to soak up as much western culture as they could. However, the visit to Constantinople by the French Empress Eugénie showed that the Turks still had much to learn, especially when it came to royal receptions. As the French imperial yacht *L'Aigle* approached the Bosphorus, a salute was fired by 30 Turkish cannon. Unfortunately, no one had told the gunners they were only supposed to fire blank rounds at their guests, and the Empress was forced to duck as cannonballs rained down around her. She survived, but her visit was made even more memorable by the Sultan's parting gift, a Turkish carpet fashioned from human hair. It made such an impression on one of Eugénie's ladies-in-waiting that she fainted.

King William III, one of the coldest, most charmless and ugliest of England's monarchs, fretted because his subjects didn't love him. One day he was highly flattered when he went out walking dressed in farmer's clothes, and bumped into a doctor along the way, who recognised the King immediately. William smiled and enquired how this had been possible. 'I know you,' the doctor replied, 'by your hump.'

The Russian Empress Anne was fond of making up new and interesting punishments to fit any crime. When, for example, she decided that two overweight noblewomen were guilty of gluttony, she had them force fed huge amounts of pastries until they almost choked to death on their own vomit. Few complained about the treatment: the Empress always had their tongues pulled out first.

Afghanistan's King Amanullah was so impressed by his first visit to London after World War I that he went straight home and passed a law compelling his male subjects to wear bowler hats.

The mad Ottoman Sultan Murad IV ordered the death penalty for anyone who was caught smoking tobacco. One of his favourite pastimes was personally sneaking up on smokers and surprising them. Wherever he travelled around Turkey, his stopping-off points were usually marked by a spate of executions of smokers. Even on the battlefield, nicotine addicts weren't safe from him. He had his own soldiers beheaded, and hanged, drawn and quartered. Failing this, he would sometimes crush their hands and feet and leave them helpless in no man's land.

When the King of Siam wanted to have some of his relatives murdered he was reminded of an inconvenient Siamese tradition which forbade the spilling of royal blood on the ground – he had them pounded to death with a large mortar and pestle instead.

King Philip II of Spain's son and heir Don Carlos was a mentally retarded psychopath who was eventually disinherited, locked up and quietly done away with. Carlos had young girls whipped for his enjoyment, animals roasted alive while he watched, and he murdered at least six men for some real or imagined slight against him. Once, when he was dissatisfied with a pair of boots that had been made for him, he had them cut into pieces and forced the cobbler to eat them. On another occasion when some water was inadvertently emptied from a house balcony and splashed near him, he had the occupants executed.

The Indian Maharajah of Jaipur declared a fifteen-mile exclusion zone around his capital where he alone was allowed to hunt. He had poachers tortured by pushing ground hot chillies into their rectums.

Czar Ivan the Terrible specialised in inventing brutal but ingenious deaths for his enemies. When the Archbishop of Novgorod was suspected of organising an uprising against him, Ivan had the entire population massacred by tossing them into a freezing river. He then had the Archbishop sewn into a bearskin and hunted to death by a pack of hounds. He had his treasurer boiled to death in a cauldron, and his imperial chancellor was strung up while members of Ivan's entourage took turns to hack pieces off him, starting with an ear.

Prince Philip, the Duke of Edinburgh, once dubbed 'the best argument for republicanism since George III', is renowned for his epic contribution to diplomacy. In France in 1969 he remarked to a local news reporter, 'Isn't it a pity Louis XVI was sent to the guillotine?' and on a visit to Canada announced, 'We don't come here for our health . . . we can think of better ways of enjoying ourselves,' a remark which resulted in the removal of his wife's head from Canadian banknotes within a matter of weeks. On Prince Philip's South American tour he told the fascist dictator of Paraguay General Alfredo Stroessner, the man who protected war criminals, 'It's a pleasant change to be in a country that isn't ruled by its people,' and in Panama when he was startled by a nearby police-car siren, he advised his escort to 'switch that bloody thing off, you silly fucker'. In China in 1986, he described his hosts as 'slitty-eyed' and said Beijing was 'ghastly'. Later that year he told the World Wildlife Fund that 'if it's got four legs and it's not a chair, if it's got two wings and it flies, but it's not an aeroplane, and if it swims and it's not a submarine, the Cantonese will eat it.' In 1993 while in Hungary, he felt obliged to point out that most Hungarians were 'pot-bellied'.

Looking Good,
Feeling Great

The *de rigueur* fashion item for both men and women in the eighteenth century was a set of mouseskin eyebrows stuck on with fish glue.

In biblical times, even a bad case of teenage acne was likely to get you branded a leper and shunned by society. This would mean, to all intents and purposes, that you would be written off as a dead man, and would have a requiem mass sung for you, as was the custom for all living lepers.

About 2000 merkins, or pubic hair wigs, are sold annually worldwide. They originally became popular when the regular treatment for venereal disease involved shaving off all the pubic hair.

Mary Queen of Scots was bald, a secret which she hid even from many of her closest acquaintances with a thick auburn wig. The first hint for many of her friends that Mary was follically challenged was only when it became horribly obvious on the day of her execution. After she had been beheaded the executioner picked up her head by the hair to show it to the crowd, and the wig came away in his hand.

Tibetans used to grow the nail on the little finger of their left hand extra-long so that they could use it to pick their ears and noses clean.

When the mother of King George I, the Electress Sophia, finally lost her teeth she replaced all her missing dentures with little squares of wax.

The Wonder of You
Demodox folliculorum has eight stumpy legs and a tail, is about one third of a millimetre long and loves nothing more than to recline in the warm, oily pits of your hair follicles. Most adults have this mite, usually on the head and especially in eyelashes, and often in nipples too.

You have close cousins of the bacteria which causes gonorrhoea living in your mouth and throat.

The last time that you could have truthfully claimed to have been clean was just before you were born. It is impossible to rid yourself completely of germs, even if you bathed in iodine or alcohol.

The average human anus expels about one pint of methane gas per day.

There is no known cure for male baldness which will leave you with your testes intact. As baldness relies upon the male testicular hormone testosterone, castration is the only answer. The side effects of castration, however, include loss of body hair, a falsetto voice, a tendency to obesity, insomnia, a weak bladder and poor eyesight.

About half of the bulk of your faeces comprises the dead bodies of bacteria which live inside your gut.

The average British adult stool weighs about four ounces. It is smaller, harder, darker, about half the size and much less likely to float than the third world equivalent.

Women's face powder in the sixteenth century was made from crushed pig bones.

In March 1983, the Danish hair-fetishist Luigi Longhi was jailed for life after he was found guilty of kidnapping, then murdering a West German girl hitchhiker. Longhi admitted that before strangling her, he had washed her hair four times.

Disraeli liked to tease Lords Malmesbury and Lyndhurst for rouging their cheeks, and mocked Palmerston because his false teeth always looked like they were falling out of his mouth when he spoke. He, however, secretly dyed his own hair.

In the eighteenth century, at the peak of wig wearing in England, male wigs became so voluminous that you needed to denude ten long-haired men to make one hairpiece – hence the expression 'big-wig'. Horace Walpole's wig was so thick and heavy that he used to remove it during debates in the House of Commons because he couldn't hear through it. Human hair was in such short supply that wigs were made from the hair of horses, goats and cows. Genuine barristers' wigs are still made from horse hair today.

For centuries, English women rubbed crushed strawberries on their bodies because they believed it would enlarge their breasts.

Samuel Pepys wrote in his diary that he had to return his brand new periwig to his barber to have it cleansed of nits. 'Which vexed me cruelly,' complained Pepys, 'that he should put such a thing in my hands.'

You little ecosystem, you . . .
You have roughly about the same number of bacteria and other organisms on your skin and hair as there are people on earth.

Ancient Egyptians tried to cure hair loss with the application of vipers' oil and bats' ears.

Caligula was so sensitive about his premature baldness that he frequently ordered men with good heads of hair to shave it all off out of spite.

The average pair of socks traps about 200 milligrams of dead skin per day.

The Ancient Egyptians used various depilatory devices to completely rid their heads and bodies of hair, including the insides of their ears and nostrils. The fashion had more to do with hygiene than masochism: the Nile valley climate was an ideal breeding ground for body bugs and lice, and shaving was the only preventive measure against bodily infestation.

King George IV's niece, the young Princess Victoria, noted in her diary that one nearly threw up when required to kiss her flatulent uncle because his cheeks were nearly half-an-inch thick with greasepaint.

Between the fourteenth and sixteenth centuries, fashionable English ladies wore fur collars called 'flea cravats', exclusively to lure fleas away from the rest of their clothes, and which could be shaken out later.

About 40 per cent of Britain's adults admit to being constipated.

In Ancient Rome, blond wigs were fashionable for both men and women. The most sought-after variety on the market was made from hair shorn from the conquered natives of Northern Europe. The wigs were not very realistic, and were often kept in place with a piece of string tied under the chin. Bald Romans who couldn't afford wigs did the next best thing and had hair painted on to their skulls instead.

Apart from the razor-blade, two indispensable implements in a gentleman's toilet routine from Roman times until the nineteenth century were the ear-scoop and the tongue-scraper.

Henry III of France, the 'King of Sodom', had long, flowing locks which he lost when still quite young after repeatedly dyeing his hair with untreated chemicals. Later he went around wearing a velvet cap which had bunches of hair sewn inside the rim. Before wigs became fashionable for men in England in the late seventeenth century, bald men would often sew clumps of hair inside the rims of their hats.

The first widely used British tooth-cleaning agent was nitric acid in solution. It may have been fatal for teeth and gums, but it definitely made your teeth whiter.

At the height of the craze for wigs for both men and women, the demand for human hair was so great that it became dangerous to let a child with a good head of hair stray out of sight.

Instead of shaving, Julius Caesar had his facial hairs individually plucked out with tweezers. Hadrian was the first Roman Emperor to make beards fashionable: he grew one to hide his scrofulous skin complaint.

Every nook of granny
Every time you bathe, the number of organisms on your skin and body actually increases by a

factor of three; the water frees them from the nooks and crannies on your body and encourages them to multiply.

Roman women made hair conditioner from bears' grease, deer's bone marrow, rats' heads and excrement.

The fashion for wearing dentures made from real human teeth went hand in hand with the rise of bodysnatching in the first half of the nineteenth century. People were prepared to wear the teeth of the dead, but they weren't too keen on giving much thought to how they got them in the first place. The Irish anatomist, Professor Macartney of Trinity College, Dublin once silenced a mob protesting about raids by bodysnatchers on their local burial ground by pointing out that many of the crowd were complaining with mouths full of teeth plundered from under their very feet. Later there was a craze not just for dentures made from human teeth, but for human teeth transplants – teeth removed from one set of gums and surgically implanted into another. Although it was dangerous, unhygienic, and encouraged poor people to sell their own perfectly good teeth for pennies, this practice didn't completely die out until shortly before World War I.

It became fashionable in sixteenth-century Italy for women to colour their teeth. In Russia they always dyed them black.

Elizabethan women drank the urine of puppy dogs to improve their complexions.

Many nineteenth-century hairstyles became verminous because they were usually set with rancid lard and stuffed with horse hair. Many women wore silver or gold wire cages on their heads at bedtime to prevent mice nesting in their tresses.

Queen Elizabeth I wore an attractive hair pomade made from a mixture of apples and puppy dog fat.

Although it lacked a certain body and shine, hair from corpses was widely used in the manufacture of wigs for 300 years. The bottom briefly fell out of the periwig business during the Great Plague of London in 1665: Samuel Pepys recorded that no one dared buy a new wig for fear that the hair had been cut from the heads of plague-infected cadavers.

The gruesome Chinese fetish for foot-binding began in the thirteenth century. China's Empress Taki was born with a club foot, and her ingratiating courtiers started to bind their own feet to imitate her. Soon, the stunted, bound female foot was considered sexy. Chinese husbands also found the fashion to be a handy way of keeping their wives faithful: foot-binding effectively crippled them, and so they were incapable of running away with another man.

Parasites can live in virtually every organ or tissue in your body, but some species target specific parts. Guinea worms live beneath your skin, roundworms go for your lungs or muscle tissue, and flukes head for your bloodstream, liver, intestine or lungs. Tapeworms flourish most happily in your intestines. Your body can easily accommodate a tapeworm up to ten metres long – the good news is that they can't breed inside you, at least not without exiting then re-entering your body. Some types of worm found in raw fish, especially fish used in Japanese *sushi*, live in your brain.

Hydatid cysts are formed by the larval stage of the tapeworm. This commonly exists in dogs, but a dog can pass it on to a human with a simple lick of the hand. Once this cyst is inside your body it can and often does swell to the size of a football.

If it weren't for the slimy mucus which lines the walls of your gut, your stomach would readily digest itself.

There are now 25 known types of venereal, or sexually

transmitted diseases which are harmful to mankind, variously caused by viruses, bacteria, parasites, mites, yeast, chlamydiae and fungi.

Every day you shed about 10,000 million skin scales into the atmosphere.

The act of continually picking your nose will consume only about ten calories an hour.

The man in your life, and the life on your man
Your armpits and groin carry the largest population of bacteria: on average, a grown man will have about one million in each armpit. This figure is known to be accurate because it is based on surgically removed skin, which is frozen then sectioned.

There are three types of lice which enjoy the pleasure of your company: *Pediculus humanus capitis* (the head louse), *Pediculus humanus corporis* (the body louse) and *Phthirus pubis* (the pubic louse, or 'crab'). The body louse likes to live in your clothes and will only venture out on to your skin when it is hungry, and then like all lice, it will feed by sucking your blood. Sexual intercourse apart, you can catch pubic lice from lavatory seats, bed linen or moulting pubic hairs.

At any one time you could be walking around with up to 155 different types of yeast colonies on your skin.

One of the most populous strains, *Pityrosporum ovale*, lives in and around your nose, with a population density of anything up to half a million per square centimetre. Dandruff sufferers tend to have a higher yeast population than other people, as do people who are taking steroids, because the drug suppresses the body's natural immune defences and encourages yeast and fungal growths. Athlete's foot is caused by a fungus – a more evolved form of yeast. In the US Air Force severe cases of athlete's foot were treated by amputating toes.

More than 90 per cent of the population are carriers of the herpes virus.

Every time you breathe in you swallow about 60,000 bacteria.

During the course of your lifetime, you will use about fifteen and a half miles of toilet paper. Or about eighteen and a half miles if you're a woman and you're using it to remove your make-up.

When the French actress Sarah Bernhardt went into hospital during World War I to have a leg amputated, the organisers of the Pan American Exposition cabled

46

her offering $100,000 to exhibit her leg. She cabled back: 'Which one?' Later she had an artificial leg designed for her by an English engineering company – the same people who made Douglas Bader's legs. She was thrilled with it until they sent her the bill, so she sent the leg back.

A Dirty Job, But
Someone Had To Do It . . .

In eighteenth-century London, before the invention of the public convenience, some people made an honest living out of the ownership of a long cloak and a bucket. They simply walked the streets until they found a desperate client, then for a specified fee wrapped the cloak around the customer and looked the other way while he shat in the bucket.

The Kray twins were once agents for Alvin Stardust.

The world's most difficult stand-up comic routine was performed by eunuch dwarfs in the employ of Turkey's Ottoman Sultans. The dwarfs were required to keep the royal womenfolk laughing while they gave birth.

Every morning without fail, Sir Astley Cooper, surgeon to George IV and the Duke of Wellington, rose between 5 and 6 a.m. and dissected two corpses before breakfast. If Sir Astley couldn't get hold of a fresh human cadaver, London Zoo would occasionally chip in with the odd elephant.

Before Austria's Emperor Franz Josef would climb into his lederhosen, his valet had to put them on to break them in.

The ultimate dead-end job
The pay is dreadful and the prospects are appalling, but at least it spares your relatives the nuisance of organising a funeral and it's good news for live baboons. Scientists investigating car safety at the University of Heidelberg have been using human crash dummies, including the bodies of dead children, for nearly 20 years. Although the use of cadavers instead of monkeys in road safety tests only occurs in Germany, experts in many other countries including the UK who say they find the tests morally repugnant still pay to see the results of them.

In 1993, a 25-year-old French dwarf earned the right to be thrown bodily across the room for a living. Manuel Wachensheim successfully appealed against a ban on the sport of 'dwarf tossing' imposed by the French government because it was degrading.

Lord Tennyson's job as Poet Laureate to Queen Victoria in 1857 was paid less than the position of royal rat-catcher.

The most grisly industrial dispute in history was the

unofficial strike by London's bodysnatchers in the nineteenth century. Spare corpses in Britain were so scarce that the few available were often salted for later use, then hung and dried like herrings. Grave robbing became a natural consequence of the law of supply and demand. Anatomists needed bodies upon which to practise, so they entered into fair agreements with the bodysnatchers; thus otherwise respectable men were forced into shady business arrangements with the very lowest of Britain's lowlife. The so-called 'king' of the London bodysnatching scene, Ben Crouch, called his men out in 1811 at the start of the lecturing season for anatomy students, to back his demand for a rise in the going rate for corpses. Unfortunately for Crouch there was no shortage of amateur grave robbers, many of them medical students, who were prepared to undermine the strike, and after just a few weeks he was forced into a hasty compromise with the surgeons and ordered his men back to work. Crouch and his gang later took their revenge by breaking into dissecting rooms and mutilating corpses supplied by the strikebreakers so that they were no longer of any use to anatomists.

Britain's premier *pétomane* is Paul Oldfield of Macclesfield, alias Mr Methane, who makes a living out of his ability to break wind to the tune of *The Flight of the Bumblebee*, and *How Much is That Doggy in the Window?* These talents, however, as well as his extraordinary ability to extinguish candles anally and to fire darts, have failed to secure him an insurance policy for his biggest asset. Various insurance brokers have turned him down on the basis that they found it impossible to put a price on his anus. Mr Methane lamented: 'I'm sitting on a fortune here and it could blow up in my face.'

Fewer people complained about dogs fouling the street in nineteenth-century England because the collection of dog faeces was a lucrative business. The latter-day human pooper-scoopers were called 'pure finders', and they sold the dung to tanners, who rubbed it into animal skins to help 'purify' them. Not surprisingly, the tanners were nearly as far down on the social scale as their suppliers. According to experts, not any old dog turd would do, and the very best tanning dung was the imported Turkish variety.

The eighteenth-century English artist Benjamin West had the body of an executed murderer crucified to see how it hung.

George II suffered dreadfully from both piles and an anal fistula, but he was very vain and notoriously touchy about his ailments, which were supposed to be a secret from everyone. When one of his Lords of the Bedchamber tactlessly enquired after the King's health, George sacked him on the spot.

When the 1940s Hollywood starlet Frances Farmer got herself arrested on a drink-driving charge, she cheerfully signed her occupation as 'cocksucker'.

Being on Peter the Great's payroll could be a tricky business. Peter once saw a bad tooth being pulled, and was suddenly consumed with a burning desire to become an amateur dentist. Overnight, the Czar's retinue of 250 courtiers became unwilling accomplices to his new hobby, as he carried out spot-checks on the mouth of anyone who happened to be passing. If any tooth looked suspect, he whipped it out. Peter was an incredibly strong man and it was not unusual for him to get carried away and accidentally remove gums as well. One day, one of his courtiers appealed to him for help: his wife had terrible toothache, he said, but she was so scared to have it pulled she would pretend nothing was wrong whenever a dentist approached her. The Czar obliged, and ignoring the screams and protests of the woman, pulled her tooth. Later it emerged that the woman had never had toothache in the first place: she'd had a major row with her husband, and he just wanted to teach her a lesson.

In the nineteenth century, alcoholism was reckoned to be more commonplace among gravediggers than in any other occupation. England's churchyards were in a terrible state, overcrowded and clogged up with bones and rotting corpses, and the poor wretches found their work so appalling that most felt it necessary to get blind drunk before they could do their job.

Belgium's nineteenth-century 'Rubber King' Leopold II, who personally owned a large chunk of central Africa, employed a gruesome incentive scheme to strip the Congo of its natural resources and increase his personal fortune. The local population was forced to collect rubber by Leopold's government agents, who were usually cannibals from local tribes, chosen by the Belgians for their expertise in human butchery. As no new rubber vines were ever planted, the commodity quickly became scarce. The Congo natives, unable to supply their quota quickly enough, were forced to work faster on pain of death by Leopold's vicious agents. These agents in turn had to prove that they had done their job properly by returning with baskets full of severed human hands taken from dead employees. When the agents were accused of being too wasteful with bullets, they cut off the hands of the living.

In seventeenth-century Britain, human ordure was known as 'gong': professional cesspit emptiers were called 'gongfarmers'.

When one of Louis XI's courtiers drew attention to the fact that the King had a flea on his lace collar and removed it for him, the King rewarded him with gold. When another of his courtiers tried to ingratiate himself with the King by repeating the same trick the following day, Louis had him flogged.

Although Louis XV was arguably the most powerful man in Europe, his grasp of economics was somewhat flawed. When he heard that the workers were starving, he sympathetically sacked 80 of his gardeners. He took them back when someone gently explained to him that he had just ensured that they too would starve.

Cool customer

US company president Robert Nelson made a living out of the dying with his cryogenics service: he preserved, in capsules of liquid nitrogen, the bodies of people who were prepared to pay large sums of money in the hope that one day science would find a cure for death. In 1981 Nelson and one of his employees, Joseph Klockgether, were successfully sued for fraud by relatives of their clients and ordered to pay $1 million in damages after admitting that they had allowed their freeze-dried loved ones to thaw out accidentally.

In 1992, six disgruntled French boy scouts went home empty-handed after labouring for two hours with scrubbing brushes to clean graffiti off the walls of the Grotte de Mayfrières, a tourist attraction in Southern France. How were they to know that they had erased 15,000-year-old cave paintings of bison?

And finally . . .

After a British court ruling in 1994, keyboard operators everywhere rejoiced as Repetitive Strain Injury joined the following recognised workplace health problems, as listed in D. Hunter's *The Diseases of Occupation*: Apple Sorters' Disease, Bakers' Eczema, Billingsgate Hump (a problem for fish porters), Boiler Makers' Deafness, Bricklayers' Itch, Bricklayers' Elbow, Bricklayers' Anaemia (clearly a bunch of hypochondriacs), Biscuit Makers' Dermatitis, Budgerigar Fanciers' Lung, Bullman's Hand (bad news for artificial inseminators), Cable Makers' Rash,

Chain Makers' Cataracts, Cigar Makers' Cramps, Cigarette Cutters' Asthma, Cobblers' Mouth, Combers' Fever, Compositors' Cramp, Confectioners' Dermatitis, Coolie Itch (afflicts paddy-field workers), Cornpickers' Pupil, Cotton Mill Fever, Cotton Twisters' Cramp, Cotton Weavers' Deafness, Covent Garden Hummy (curvature of the spine), Dairyman's Itch (caused by a form of VD found in cows, horses and sometimes dogs), Deal Runners' Shoulder (a big problem for timber porters), Diamond Cutters' Cramps, Dockers' Itch, Dustman's Shoulder, Farmers' Lung, Feather Pluckers' Disease, Fireman's Eye (afflicts potters who fire kilns, not firemen), Fish Handlers' Disease, Florists' Cramps, French Polishers' Dermatitis, Gold Smelters' Cataracts, Footballers' Migraine (headaches and visual field defects, according to Hunter, caused by repeated blows to the head), Fish Handlers' Disease, Glassworkers' Cataract, Grocers' Itch, Harpists' Cramps, Hatters' Tremor, Hodman's Shoulder, Labourers' Spine (osteoarthritis), Miners' Bunches (hookworm, also known as Tile Makers' or Tunnellers' Disease), Miners' Cramps, Miners' Elbow, Mushroom Workers' Lung, Nailmakers' Cramps, Nuns' Bursitis,

Paddy-field Foot, Paprika-splitters' Lung, Printers' Asthma, Pork Finger (afflicts abbatoir workers), Potters' Asthma, Potters' Rot (severe lead poisoning from glazes handled in the manufacture of ceramic tiles: one employer in North Staffordshire tried to cure it by brewing free-issue beer laced with sulphuric acid for the workforce), Poultry Pluckers' Finger, Seal Finger (unique to sealers and whalers), Shipyard

Conjunctivitis, Shoemakers' Cramps, Sugar Cane Cutters' Cramps, Swineherds' Disease, Tailors' Ankle, Tea Tasters' Cough, Telegraphists' Cramp, Tripe Scrapers' Disease, Tulip Finger (afflicts market gardeners), Upholsterers' Mouth, Wool Sorters' Disease (anthrax, also known in France as 'Bradford Disease'), and alphabetically last but by no means least, Weavers' Bottom.

Unnatural Causes

The following all met their deaths in a rather unfortunate manner . . .

Queen Eleanor (wife of Edward I): blood poisoning after sucking the pus out of her husband's septic wound.

Emperor Menelik II of Ethiopia: misadventure. He was convinced that whenever he fell ill he could cure himself by eating pages from the Bible. In 1913 he had a stroke and later died while attempting to eat the entire Book of Kings.

Viscount Palmerston (British Prime Minister 1855–8, 1859–65): heart attack while having sex with a young parlour-maid on his billiard table on 18 October 1865.

Sir Arthur Aston (Royalist commander during the Civil War): beaten to death with his own wooden leg by Cromwell's men.

George I: apoplexy, after bingeing on melons. After hearing of his ex-wife's death he went to watch a play, then set out for her burial with one of his mistresses in tow. It was on this same trip to Germany that he died in his coach.

Catherine the Great, George II and Elvis Presley: heart failure on the toilet while straining to overcome constipation. The King (George II that is, not Elvis), according to his long-suffering German *valet de chambre*, was a loud and frequent farter. On this occasion however, he heard a roar which he judged to be 'louder than the usual royal wind' and found George slumped dead on the floor.

Demetrius Myiciura (Polish emigrant living in Stoke-on-Trent): choked to death on garlic in 1973 while attempting to ward off vampires. The coroner noted that although Stoke was not particularly renowned for vampirism, the deceased had, shortly after moving there, formed the view that you never could be too careful, and regularly slept with a clove of garlic in his mouth.

Nelson Rockefeller (US Vice-president): heart attack at the age of 71 whilst copulating with his mistress.

Oscar Wilde: an abscess of the brain which had spread from his infected ear after an expensive operation by a celebrated ear specialist. When Wilde was told how much the failed operation had cost, he sighed,

'Oh well then, I suppose I shall have to die beyond my means.' According to another even wittier but apocryphal version, his last words were, 'Either that wallpaper goes, or I do.'

King Alexander of Greece: blood poisoning after being bitten by his pet monkey.

King Alexander and Queen Drago of Serbia: shot, hacked to pieces with swords, their skulls bashed in with rifle butts, then tossed out of an upper floor window into the garden. They got in the way of a palace coup.

Queen Anne, George IV and William IV: cirrhosis of the liver due to alcoholism. George IV was very badly embalmed and his body became so swollen that it almost burst through the lead lining in his coffin. It was finally necessary for someone to drill a hole in it and let out some of the putrid air. His death was exactly like his reign, as eye-witness Mrs Arbuthnot recorded, altogether a thoroughly unpleasant experience. The *Times* wrote, 'There was never an individual less regretted by his fellow creatures than this deceased King.'

Arthur Mandelko (24-year-old Superman fan): froze to death in his fridge while dressed as Superman.

Mandelko had been in there for about a month, dressed as his favourite superhero, when his landlord found his frozen corpse in 1970. The landlord explained that his lodger had long believed he was Superman and spent most evenings jumping from one roof to another. He was forced to stop this activity when neighbours complained about the thumping sounds. Police theorised that Mandelko's planned escape by using his super-heated X-ray vision had somehow gone wrong.

King James II of Scotland: in battle in 1460 when one of his own cannons exploded and a piece of shrapnel sliced off the top of his head.

Girolamo Cardano (Italian mathematician and astrologer): suicide. Cardano was renowned as a sort of sixteenth-century Russell Grant and drew up horoscopes for the crowned heads of Europe, including England's young King Edward VI. Success went to Cardano's head, and he predicted his own death, down to the very hour. When the time arrived and Cardano found himself in robust good health, he topped himself rather than be proved wrong.

Arnold Bennett: typhoid. He couldn't resist showing off by drinking a glass of Paris tap water in 1931 to demonstrate how perfectly safe it was.

Pope Alexander VI: arsenic poisoning, after inadvertently drinking from a poisoned cup he had had prepared for his cardinals. His body swelled up until it was too big for his made-to-measure coffin, and the porters only succeeded in getting him in there by rolling him up in a carpet, stuffing it in the coffin then pounding it with their fists.

Elagabalus (Roman Emperor): murdered on the toilet, then his body was thrown down a sewer.

Isadora Duncan (American dancer): misadventure. She had just taken delivery of a brand new Bugatti racing car and wanted to show it off. She stepped into it for the first time, waved gaily to her friends, and sped away. As she did so her long red scarf became entangled in the spokes of her rear nearside wheel: it snapped her neck, killing her instantly.

Manichaeus (physician to the King of Persia): flayed alive and fed to the royal dogs, after failing to cure the King's son.

Christine Chubbock (US TV newsreader): suicide by shooting herself live in front of the cameras while she was reading the news. It emerged later that she had scripted her suicide so as not to disrupt the TV schedule.

Pope John XII: bludgeoned to death by the cuckolded husband of the woman he was having it away with at the time.

The Singing Nun: suicide. Proof that the devil really does have all the best tunes came in the form of Sister Luc-Gabrielle, a Belgian nun with an acoustic guitar, who was tragically never quite able to repeat the success of her unexpected smash hit single of 1963, *Dominique*. She did, however, come up with a million-selling album featuring such classics as *Mets Ton Joli Jupon* (Put On Your Pretty Skirt) and *J'ai Trouvé Le Seigneur* (I Have Found the Lord), shortly before her chart career was inexplicably eclipsed by Beatlemania.

Ludwig Van Beethoven: hepatic cirrhosis of the liver as a result of alcoholism, at the age of 57. Before he expired he cheerily announced, 'Wine is both necessary and good for me.'

Terry Kath (guitarist with US rock band Chicago): trying to amuse his party guests by pointing what he thought was an empty gun at his head and pulling the trigger.

Jimi Hendrix, Jim Morrison and Janis Joplin: suffocated on their own vomit.

Jean-Baptiste Lully (French composer): gangrene, after accidentally stabbing himself in the foot with his baton.

Pope Adrian IV (aka Nicholas Breakspear, the only English Pope): choked to death after accidentally swallowing a fly.

Allan Pinkerton (founder of the Pinkerton Detective Agency): gangrene, after tripping and biting his tongue.

Honoré de Balzac: caffeine poisoning, due to his habit of 50 cups of coffee per day.

Jim Fixx (American who started the jogging craze): dropped dead while jogging.

Friedrich Nietzsche: syphilis of the brain, after catching VD in a brothel in 1865.

Caroline of Brunswick-Wolfenbüttel (wife of George IV): constipation, despite being force-fed so much castor oil that 'it would have turned the stomach of a horse.'

Edmund Ironside (Saxon King): irritable bowel syndrome. His reign was curtailed when he sat on his wooden lavatory and an assassin hiding in the pit below twice thrust his longsword up the King's backside.

Maximilian I (Emperor of Mexico): his face shot off by a revolutionary firing squad full of very poor marksmen in 1867. Afterwards, parts of his body were auctioned off to souvenir hunters.

Pope Leo VIII: heart attack while having sexual intercourse.

Tiberius (Roman Emperor): suffocation. When the 78-year-old Emperor fell ill and lapsed into a coma, everyone thought that he was dead. Just as the court officials were congratulating his young nephew and successor Caligula, Tiberius sat up and asked for a drink. Caligula sent his chamberlain in to finish the job off by smothering the old man with his bedclothes.

Love Hurts

The Roman Emperor Elagabalus, although he married five times in four years, was sexually confused. He liked to dress up and pretend he was a female prostitute, and set aside a room in his palace where he would hide behind a curtain and solicit passers-by. His unfortunate 'clients' were expected not only to humour him, but also to pay well for the privilege.

The patron saint of syphilitics, St Denis, is also the namesake of Paris's celebrated centre of prostitution, Rue St Denis.

Russia's Czar Peter the Great had an awesome libido which he sated with anyone who happened to be passing, irrespective of sex or age. He paid the Saxon artist Danhauer to paint nude portraits of his favourite page boys, and once startled the visiting Duke of Holstein by grabbing him by the ears and shoving his tongue down his throat. One of the Czar's lovers, Abraham Hannibal, was known at court as 'the negro of Peter the Great'. He had originally been bought in a Turkish slave market and given to Peter as a gift. Pushkin reported that their relationship was so intimate that

Peter once removed a tapeworm from Abraham's anus with his own hands. 'The anecdote is rather dirty,' noted Pushkin, 'but it gives a good picture of Peter's habits.'

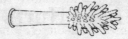

Oral contraceptives, as prescribed by the ancient Chinese, took the form of sixteen tadpoles fried in quicksilver to be swallowed in rapid succession.

When Louis XIV began to tire of his mistress Madame de Montespan, she tried to revive his interest by feeding him an aphrodisiac made of toad excrement.

Paris in the nineteenth century was such a hotbed of prostitution that for virtually every great artist and writer who lived and worked there, life-threatening social diseases were accepted as an occupational hazard. Renoir once fretted that he couldn't possibly be a genius because, unlike Manet, Maupassant, Dumas and Baudelaire, he hadn't yet caught syphilis.

The most common cause of death for South American women under 50 is illegal abortion.

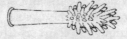

The term 'clap' is derived from the sixteenth-century French *clappoir*, which describes the bubo or groin swellings sported by gonorrhoea sufferers.

If the cap fits . . .

Cabbage, sweet basil, half a lemon, tar and onion juice have all been used down the ages for their supposed contraceptive qualities. The celebrated Islamic physician Avicenna recommended that women who wanted to avoid pregnancy should jump backwards seven or nine times immediately after sexual intercourse. A prominent Dominican theologian and birth control expert in the thirteenth century wrote a treatise on contraception, which stated that a woman would not become pregnant if she spat three times in the mouth of a frog, or if she ate bees. He was of course absolutely correct, providing she didn't have sex either.

In 1916, the Viennese professor Ludwig Steinach hit upon a theory that the male vasectomy had the effect of the fabled elixir of youth: one snip and a man's ageing processes would stop, his hair grow thicker and his sexual potency increase. In the years that followed, thousands of men underwent 'Steinaching' – including his near neighbour, Sigmund Freud – until the Professor was forced to admit that he'd got it slightly wrong. All that his patients could in fact look forward to was impotence, serious long-term psychological problems including depression, and a lifetime of ill health caused by a series of complications, one of which was testicular cancer.

Queen Victoria's consort Prince Albert gave his name to a form of body piercing, fashionable among Victorian gentlemen, whereby an erection could be restrained by a device made of little hoops.

Thanks largely to England's public school system which, in the seventeenth and eighteenth centuries, was a charter for sodomites, the English acquired a reputation across Europe for homosexuality which lasted for centuries. In spite of this, English laws against homosexuality have always been more severe than anywhere else. In 1553, Henry VIII introduced hanging to punish 'the detestable and abominable Vice of Buggery committed with mankind or beast'. In France, homosexuality and flagellation are still referred to as *le vice anglais* – 'the English vice'.

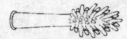

Siberian women used to flirt with the opposite sex by lobbing slugs at them.

Paul Gauguin's most lasting contribution to Tahiti was syphilis. Some of his best-known paintings were executed there while trying to find a cure for his condition in the sun.

Porcupines are cable of scx about ten times a night, all year round.

Between his first encounter with Dr Johnson in 1763 and his death 35 years later, James Boswell caught gonorrhoea nineteen times. His first dose came from a minor actress named Sally Forrester. Although Boswell was a strict Calvinist Presbyterian, he continued to sleep with prostitutes long after his marriage in 1769, and fathered five bastards. In Boswell's day, gonorrhoea was a much more painful and debilitating disease than it is now, and the only recognised treatment up until the last century involved inserting curved metal rods into the penis.

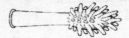

Frederick the Great, who never once slept with his wife, was rumoured in later years to have been romantically attached to his pack of Italian whippet bitches.

Oscar Wilde suffered from tertiary syphilis, and was renowned for his mouthful of rotten teeth, which could have been a symptom either of the disease itself, or of the mercury treatment he took for it. His novel *The Picture of Dorian Gray* was an allegory of his disease. The horrible illness Gray suffers from, the 'leprosies of sin', turn him into 'a monstrous and loathsome thing' with 'hideous face', 'misshapen body', 'failing limbs', 'warped lips' and 'coarse bloated hands'.

For a randy squirrel monkey, foreplay involves urinating in your partner's face.

The actress Sarah Bernhardt claimed a unique treble by sleeping with Edward VII, his bisexual son and heir 'Eddy' the Duke of Clarence, and the French Emperor Napoleon III. The favourite gossip around London at the time was that Ms Bernhardt and Edward VII enjoyed copulating in a special silk-lined coffin which she kept in her bedroom for special 'guests'. Given the

King's elephantine girth it was a fair bet that she was on top while Edward played dead.

Nineteenth-century gynaecologists advised women that the quickest route to fertility was to eat a pregnant rabbit, foetus and all.

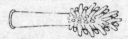

Condoms have been widely available since the Renaissance when slaughterhouse workers made sheaths from sausage skins. They were originally used as they are today – as a barrier against disease, not as a contraceptive. The alleged inventor Colonel Condom, who is said to have been so coy about his discovery that he had his name changed, is an entirely mythical character.

The Ottoman Sultan Suleiman I 'The Magnificent' had a harem of 900 women, even though he was gay.

During the British Raj, more than half the British troops serving in India suffered from venereal disease, so commanding officers set about organising army-run brothels containing only infection-free whores. Army quartermasters received requisitions which read: 'Please send young and attractive women.' The officer classes, however, as ex-public schoolboys, had other diversions. A popular refrain in the mess lamented: 'There is a boy across the river with a bottom like a peach, but alas I cannot swim.'

Saudi Arabia's first King, Ibn-Saud, is reputed to have had sex with three different women every night from the age of eleven until his death in 1953 aged 72.

Although syphilis has been around for thousands of years it only took root in Europe about four centuries ago, when it was first officially catalogued as 'painful pustules on the reproductive organs spreading to the body and face, black pustules, carbuncles, rashes, ulcers, buboes, painfully swollen joints, fever, lassitude, rotting flesh, blindness and lingering death.' The origins of the disease were a matter of fierce national pride: Frenchmen called it the Naples or the Italian Disease; Italians, the British and the Spanish called it the French Pox; the Russians and the Germans called it the Polish Disease; the Poles called it the German Disease; the Portuguese called it the Dutch Pox; the Persians and the Japanese called it the Portuguese Disease; and virtually everyone else called it the Turkish Disease. No one thought of calling it the West Indian Disease, which was after all where Columbus and his syphilitic, itchy crew had imported it from.

The nineteenth-century poet Charles Swinburne admitted he once copulated with a monkey which was dressed in women's clothing.

Most of the people in the Bible who are described as lepers were probably syphilitic. The outward signs of advanced syphilis are very similar to those found on lepers, and biblical 'leprosy' was nearly always described as a highly contagious disease – a description inappropriate to leprosy but which fits syphilis perfectly. Unlike syphilis, leprosy requires prolonged body contact and a healthy person can live amongst lepers for years without becoming infected. Herod, King of Judaea probably suffered from syphilitic insanity: he was described as having private parts which were 'putrefied and eaten up with worms'.

For services rendered to an isolated garrison of troops in the late 1940s during the war in Indo-China, France awarded two prostitutes the *Croix de Guerre*.

During World War I the British Army suffered 415,891 VD casualties.

Coloured, scented, textured and even flavoured condoms are not a recent invention. At the beginning of the eighteenth century Mrs Phillips of Leicester Square, London sold a range of prophylactics designed for the more discerning gentleman about town, including condoms hand-fashioned on glass moulds, in sheep or goat gut, pickled and scented. Some of the more exclusive variety were tied on at the neck with ribbons available in a variety of regimental colours. For extra-safe sex, however, Mrs Phillips offered her 'Superfine Double'. This double-strength contraption, about eight inches long, was advertised in *The Tatler* as 'an engine for the prevention of harms by love-adventurers'. Although condoms made from offal were all the rage in early eighteenth-century London, they were heavy and expensive passion killers and many people preferred to use the old linen variety, which needed to be dampened first (James Boswell used to wet his by dipping them in Hyde Park canal). Linen sheaths were also more economical because unlike the sheep gut variety, you could take them to the condom laundrette in St Martin's Lane. Condom sales didn't really get a lift until Mr Goodyear vulcanised rubber in 1843.

Arthur Schopenhauer, Heinrich Heine and Casanova all had syphilis, as did Peter the Great, Frederick the Great, Queen Cleopatra, and the Roman Emperors Tiberius, Marcus Aurelias, Commodus and Julius Caesar, along with his favourite bedfellow Mamuria. Julius Caesar was rampantly bisexual and may also have passed it on to the Egyptian Queen Cleopatra, who gave him a son, and Nicomedes, the warror King of Bithynia.

The Romanian dictator Nicolae Ceauçescu tried to double his country's population, thereby promoting economic growth, by completely banning all forms of contraception. Romanian women were forced to undergo monthly body searches to prove that they weren't secretly using contraceptive devices.

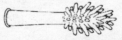

Lord Byron had sex with his nanny when he was nine years old.

Casanova tried out the very latest condoms made from animal intestine, but didn't like using them. He placed his faith in a technique by which he inserted three gold balls in his partner, purchased from a Genoese goldsmith for about £50, a method which he claimed had served him well for fifteen years. A more likely explanation for his run of luck is that he was infertile.

Femidomus Romanus
Roman women wore contraceptives made from goats' bladders.

Like most Bourbons, the French King Louis XV had an unnaturally high sex drive, but he was frightened stiff of catching syphilis. This was why he preferred to sleep with very young girls, some only fourteen years old, and would often bed several little *grisettes* at a time. Before he died on 10 May 1774, Louis made his first confession to a priest for 38 years: a courtier timed it at a full sixteen minutes.

First Among Equals

Apart from being the first to lose his head, Louis XVI was also the first French King to use a knife and fork, take a regular bath or brush his teeth.

Ronald Reagan was the first President of the United States to have his nasal polyps discussed on live TV.

George Bush was the first US President to be seen throwing up on live TV.

The first amputation ever carried out under anaesthetic was performed on 7 November 1846 in Massachusetts General Hospital, when a 21-year-old servant girl, Alice Mohan, was separated from her right leg. The operation was performed by Dr George Haywood, assisted by Andrew Morton and his astonishing new invention the ether inhaler. When the amputation was successfully completed, Haywood was understandably pleased with himself and couldn't resist a certain amount of showing off. He leaned over the girl and said, 'I guess you've been asleep Alice.' The patient replied, 'I think I have, sir.' 'Well, you know why we brought you here,' said Haywood. 'Are you ready?'. The girl replied that she was, at which Haywood plucked the leg from the sawdust where it lay and waved it triumphantly under her nose, saying, 'It's all done, Alice.' Her reply is not on record.

Earl John Russell (Prime Minister, 1846–52 and 1865–6) was the first British premier known to have taken a regular bath.

Russia's first ever book of etiquette was published in 1718 by the Romanov Empress Anne, a female psychopath who nevertheless had revolutionary ideas about good manners and wanted to keep up with European standards of good taste. Entitled *The Honest Mirror of Youth*, the slim volume advised discerning Russians how to use a knife and fork, when not to spit on the floor, not to blow their noses by applying a digit to one nostril while blowing down the other, and not to jab their elbows into their seating partners during formal dinners nor place their feet in guests' dishes while standing on the dining table.

In 1959 Bertha Dlugi of Milwaukee, USA, became the first and only person to realise the major commercial possibilities of a bird nappy which would allow pet birds to fly freely around the house without depositing their droppings.

The Frenchman Dr Phillipe Curtius opened the forerunner to the Chamber of Horrors, the *Caverne de Grands Voleurs* in 1783, and taught his talented young apprentice Madame Tussaud how to model wax. One of her first jobs was to make wax likenesses from decapitated heads removed from victims of the guillotine. Curtius acquired his models for her to work on by hanging around in cemeteries waiting for the arrival of carts containing the bodies. When Louis XV's former mistress, Madame du Barry, was executed, he rummaged through the cart for her head, oiled her face, and applied a plaster mask before tossing it into the communal grave.

King Louis XIII of France had his first wash on his seventh birthday.

On 1 July 1966, Mao Tse-tung became the first senile septuagenarian to claim a world swimming record. The Chinese leader was reported to have smashed the existing record when he swam ten miles of the river Yangtze in one hour. His doctor now thinks it is safe to admit privately that as Mao was too fat to sink or swim, if he completed the journey at all – which is incredibly unlikely – it was because he was swept along by the strong river current and couldn't get out.

An interesting variation on the more conventional electoral processes was observed in the Swedish town of Hurdenburg. Once a year, the town's worthiest bearded personages would sit around a table, allowing their beards to rest on it. A head louse was then dropped in the middle, and the owner of the beard into

77

which it chose to climb got to be mayor for the next twelve months.

Shakespeare was the first person to use the word 'bog'.

Anaesthesia by nitrous oxide – 'laughing gas' – was discovered in 1884 by Horace Wells, a young dentist living in Connecticut. Wells didn't stick around long enough to enjoy the full rewards of his marvellous discovery. He became a hopeless chloroform junkie, and one day while he was high on the drug he ran into the street and doused two passing prostitutes with acid. Wells killed himself before his case came to trial.

The Belgian anatomist Vesalius was the first surgeon who could truthfully say that he knew more about the innards of a human being than the average butcher. He got his first corpse to practise on by stealing the body of a hanged man from outside the city walls of Louvain.

Richard II was the first British King to blow his nose in a handkerchief.

Peter the Great was the first Russian Czar ever to travel west, but shortly before he left, he arranged a small exhibition to concentrate the hearts and minds of his people in case any of them had any treasonable ideas while he was away. He had the ringleaders of a suspected plot against his life arrested and tortured, then publicly dismembered and beheaded. The

Czar then ordered the remains of a famous dissident, Ivan Miloslavsky, who had been executed twelve years earlier, to be disinterred. Miloslavsky's decomposed corpse was dragged by pigs to the place of execution, butchered into small segments, then placed underneath the scaffold in an open coffin. On the platform above, the current plotters were slowly dismembered so that their fresh blood irrigated the remains of the late Miloslavsky below. The severed body parts were neatly arranged in a large, human meat pie, and their heads fixed on spikes. Peter left express orders that no one was to remove the grisly display, which lay rotting and stinking until his return.

Exhibits at the first Great Exhibition at Crystal Palace included an 'alarm bed' which catapulted the sleeper across the room at a chosen hour, and a physician's walking stick whose handle doubled as an enema-inducer.

In 1993, Queen Elizabeth II became the first British monarch since Queen Victoria to volunteer to pay income tax. According to her tax return, she is poorer than Mick Jagger.

The sixteenth-century French surgeon Ambroise Paré earned the dying and, on a very good day, the undying gratitude of his patients when he became the first doctor to realise that it wasn't really necessary to cauterise an open wound by pouring oil onto it, or to stem bleeding during amputation using a red hot iron.

The first circuses were put on by Assyrian and Babylonian kings, but they had very limited entertainment value. Usually the one and only attraction was the sight of up to a hundred very hungry lions being let loose on a crowd of Bedouin prisoners.

The Atlanta pharmacist John Pemberton first stumbled across the original recipe for Coca-Cola in 1886 while he was working on a series of patent medicines and hair restorers which he was confident were going to make him his fortune. They included Triplex Liver Pills, Indian Queen Hair Dye and Globe of Flower Cough Syrup.

The dodo was the first known species to have been made extinct by man. The bird, unique to the island of Mauritius, wasn't killed for its meat, which was tough and bitter-tasting, but was wiped out just for kicks. Bored sailors quickly discovered that the bird was an easy target: it wouldn't run, couldn't fly and so the obvious thing to do was kill it. The last dodo was clubbed to death by a Dutch seaman in 1680.

The first man to observe human parasites was the Dutchman Anton van Leeuwenhoek, who peered through a microscope one day and found them romping in his own diarrhoeic stools. Leeuwenhoek upset some of the more sensitive gentlemen in the Royal Society with his brusque announcement: 'There are more animals in the scum of a man's teeth than there are in a whole kingdom.' His fellow scientists were even more sceptical when the Dutchman, who used as his international standard of measurement 'the eye of a louse', correctly observed that there were about eight million bacteria in every drop of drinking water.

One of the earliest inventions lodged at the British Patents Office was a device for flushing out the Loch Ness monster with a series of electric shocks.

Gaining his inspiration from the well-known sixteenth century saying that the world would beat a path to the door of the man who could build a better rack, Sir Leonard Skeffington, Lieutenant of the Tower of London, invented the most ingenious method of torture ever created by an Englishman. The regular rack was a large heavy device, awkward to use, which took up a lot of space and couldn't easily be transported. In 1534 Skeffington came up with a cunning little contraption which folded the victim in on himself, rather like a human trouser press. The whole body would be slowly folded in two until the victim's chest burst and his lifeblood was squeezed out of his hands and feet, or he confessed, whichever came first. The device became known as Skeffington's Daughter.

The Distressing Case of Queen Caroline's Bowels, and Other Matters

George II's wife Queen Caroline could swear like a trooper, but she showed remarkable composure in 1737 when she was at the receiving end of a badly bungled attempt to cure her neglected strangulated hernia. A little while after her operation, as she lay in bed surrounded by courtiers, her strangulated bowel burst open, showering a torrent of excrement all over the bed and the floor. After an embarrassed silence, one of her courtiers said she hoped the relief would do her majesty some good. The Queen replied that she hoped so too, because that was the last evacuation she would ever have. Upon her death soon afterwards, Alexander Pope was moved to write:

> Here lies wrapt in forty thousand towels
> The only proof that Caroline had bowels.

When Pepsi Cola was first introduced to China, the company's advertising executives opted to stick with their tried and trusted award-winning slogan, 'Come alive with Pepsi'. Unfortunately it lost a little something in the translation, and the product was launched before one in four of the world's population with the memorable line, 'Pepsi brings your ancestors back from the grave'.

Dead certs

The members of White's gentlemen's club in London were once famous for their willingness to bet on anything, whether it moved or not. One night a man fell motionless on the club doorstep, and by the time he had been carried in, bets had already been taken on whether or not he was stone dead.

George II was also an inveterate gambler: he lost his appetite for bookmakers when he found out that his subjects were laying bets at odds of 10–1 that he would be dead within the year.

The Forbidden City of Beijing was populated almost entirely by eunuchs. As Confucian tradition required that in order to go to heaven the whole body must be buried, the eunuchs kept their sex organs in little brine-filled jars which they carried on their person at all times. A lucrative trade in black market spares existed for anyone who had misplaced their own private parts.

The Romanov Czars were considered so sacred that in some parts of Russia post office employees were afraid to overstamp the image of Nicholas II's head.

Although the precise figures will never be known, it is likely that Mao Tse-tung killed more people than Stalin and Hitler combined. Discounting political leaders, the world's most prolific mass murderer was a member of the Indian Thuggee cult named Behram. At his trial he was convicted of strangling 931 people over a 50-year period, with the same little strip of cloth.

Percy Bysshe Shelley loathed cats: he once tied one to a kite in a thunderstorm to see if it would be electrocuted.

When Catherine the Great travelled south to visit the Crimea her aides were involved in massive subterfuge to ensure that she didn't have to put up with the bothersome business of looking at miserable, poverty-stricken subjects. Her aide and lover Gregory Potemkin stage-managed the trip so that there was not a single slum or shabby beggar in sight. Thin or unhealthy-looking individuals were sent packing and their crumbling hovels demolished, replaced by façades of freshly-painted wood, attended by happy, smiling actors. As soon as the Empress had passed by, the peasants were allowed to return, but many died in the upheaval. The 'Potemkin village' experience will not be entirely unfamiliar today to anyone who has seen at first hand a visit by a member of the British royal family, who also rule over a land smelling eternally of fresh paint, with strategically placed, well-scrubbed homeless people or chirpy punk rockers with vivid tattoos to provide colourful photo opportunities. One day when Prince Charles visited the BBC offices in Glasgow, the local corporation chiefs made an executive decision to give their lavatory a facelift with a brand new mahogany seat, just in case. When Charles had gone they decided that it would be in bad taste to let a mere commoner use the royal seat, thereby tainting it with a non-royal posterior, and so it was replaced with a new but altogether cheaper plastic version.

I have a little list
Some South American cannibals believed you could cure a limp by eating someone else's good leg.

The typical greeting of Masai tribesmen is to spit at each other.

Inmates on Death Row in Bangkok Gaol complained in 1983 that the sub-machine-gun used for dawn executions was too noisy and was making them lose sleep. The considerate governor obliged by purchasing a silencer.

President Bill Clinton shares a distinction with Saddam Hussein and Iran's mullahs: they are the only political leaders in the world to preside over states which execute the insane and mentally ill. After being reprieved four times on the day of his execution, the American murderer Robert Alton Harris went to the gas-chamber in 1992, even though his prosecutors knew that he had been brain-damaged from birth by his mother's alcohol abuse. His final request was that everyone on San Quentin's death row be treated to ice-cream. In January 1992, the mentally retarded Ricky Ray Rector was killed by lethal injection. While his executioners struggled for an hour to find the vein, Rector tried to help them. America is also the only member state of the United Nations that executes juveniles: at the end of 1992, about 30 juvenile offenders were on death row.

King George VI's birthday, 14 December, is cheerfully known to the royal family as 'Mausoleum Day' because it was the anniversary of the death by cancer of Prince Albert and the death of Albert's third child Princess Alice some seventeen years later.

In 1992, Namibia's President Nujoma appealed for foreign aid after his country's worst drought this century, then blew £16 million of it on a private plane.

Since 1979, there have been more children killed by guns on the streets of the US than there were American troops killed in Vietnam.

The most grossly misguided act of philanthropy of all time was the last will and testament of the mad miser

John Camden Neild. He left his entire fortune of almost half a million pounds (£27 million at today's value) to Queen Victoria, who was already by far the richest woman in the country. She and Prince Albert kept every penny while continuing to beg the government for a bigger Civil List, and were thus able to provide the platform upon which the current royal family's personal fortune is now based. Her envious uncle, the Belgian King Leopold I, wrote to congratulate her on her windfall. 'Such things,' he drooled, 'only still happen in England.'

A warm maggot is a happy wriggling maggot, and a fisherman will often keep a couple under his tongue just to keep them at an ambient temperature. Hence the saying, 'Old fishermen never die, they just smell that way.'

During anti-papist demonstrations in the seventeenth and eighteenth centuries, people entertained themselves by putting live cats inside effigies of the Pope, which were then set ablaze. The tortured animals would give out screams which, to everyone's amusement, appeared to come from the dummy Pope's mouth.

Thanks to the Waltham Black Act, the most notorious piece of legislature on the subject of capital punishment ever, the number of offences punishable by death in England by the early nineteenth century was more severe than anywhere else in the world. Added to the already impressive list of offences for which one could be hanged were the heinous crimes of 'associating with gypsies'; 'writing on Westminster bridge'; 'impersonating a pensioner of Greenwich Hospital'; 'writing a threatening letter'; 'appearing on the highway with a sooty face'; 'damaging a fish-pond'; or 'cutting down a tree'. In 1800, a ten-year-old boy was hanged for 'secreting notes in a post office', and in 1801, a thirteen-year-old boy was hanged for stealing a spoon.

In 1994, the cost of a pair of fashion sports shoes as worn by the average Western teenager would have fed a starving Third World family of four for six months.

Documents released for the first time under the USA's Freedom of Information Act revealed that the CIA had trained cats to carry bombs, used otters to plant underwater explosives, and spent hundreds of thousands of dollars on research into whether or not plants could be used to spy on people.

The bubonic plague never actually went away. There are several cases of plague reported every year, and some western parts of the USA are still regarded as plague risk areas. The last major outbreak of bubonic plague took place in Eastern Siberia in 1910, killing 60,000 people in 7 months. It was spread by a fur trapper who had picked it up from the skin of an infected marmot – a rodent whose pelt was sold as a substitute for sable. As recently as 1966 there were over 1000 confirmed cases, and at least 500 plague deaths in Vietnam.

In sixteenth-century England it was usual for men to greet female guests by fondling their breasts – providing they were related.

One of the senior commanders of the British troops during the Peninsular War, Sir William Erskine, was certifiably insane and had twice been confined to lunatic asylums. When the Duke of Wellington heard that Erskine was going to be fighting alongside him, he received the news with stunned disbelief, and wrote to the Military Secretary in London for an explanation. The Secretary replied, 'No doubt he is a little mad at intervals, but in his lucid intervals he is an uncommonly clever fellow, and I trust he will have no fit during the campaign, although I must say he looked a little mad as he embarked.' During one of Erskine's less lucid intervals he was found at dinner when he should have been defending a strategically important bridge. He eventually sent five men to defend it: when a fellow officer queried his decision Erskine thought better of it and sent a whole regiment, but pocketed the instruction and forgot all about it. Sir William's mental health wasn't his only problem. His eyesight was so poor that before a battle he had to ask someone to point him in the general direction of the battlefield. He eventually committed suicide by jumping out of a window in Lisbon. Found dying on the pavement, he asked bystanders: 'Why on earth did I do that?'

When Alexander the Great died, his body was preserved in a large jar of honey.

Before Hollywood's filmmakers were forced to submit to the 'Cruelty to Animals' code enforced by the American Humane Association, animals were routinely maimed and slaughtered in the name of popular entertainment. In Schaffner's film *Patton*, a donkey was clubbed to death, two calves were killed and two mules died. When an explosive device tied to a horse's chest went off, the film crew were alleged to have taken a lunch break while the horse died in agony. In the $20 million flop *Heaven's Gate*, at least five horses were killed, one of them literally blown apart, because the writer/director Michael Cimino wanted 'real blood' and banned the AHA from his set. In Sergei Dandarchuk's *Waterloo* starring Rod Steiger, *Variety* magazine reported on 'ditches clogged with dead horses'. In *Pat Garrett and Billy the Kid*, many horses died immediately or had to be put down later because of the injuries they suffered, and live chickens were buried up to their necks in the sand and used for target practice. In Francis Ford Coppola's *Apocalypse Now*, a live water buffalo was hacked to death. Ingmar Bergman once wanted to kill a live horse on the set, but when the actor David Carradine vehemently protested, Bergman had it killed off the set and filmed the still warm carcass. Bergman was also alleged to have killed three other horses, including one which was burned alive, and once had a dog strangled.

In thirteenth- and fourteenth-century England, treason against a king or nobleman was considered to be the worst possible crime: accordingly, hanging was considered much too mild a deterrent for traitors. After Simon de Montfort was killed at Evesham in 1265, his limbs were hacked off and sent to various parts of the kingdom, while his head and testicles were parcelled up and sent to the wife of one of his enemies. The rebel William Wallace got the full treatment in 1305: he was dragged through the streets of London behind a horse, then hanged, but taken down from the scaffold while he was still alive. Then his entrails were cut out and burned, and he was quartered and decapitated. His arms and legs were sent to Scotland, while his head was mounted on London Bridge.

When Henry VIII was interred in the royal vault at Windsor, a workman removed one of his finger-bones and used it to make a knife handle.

The Brazilian Cubeo tribe, who ate anyone who disagreed with them, always presented the penis and scrotum of the victim to the warrior's wife so she could eat them to make her fertile.

Nearer My Dog Than Thee . . .
To circumvent a French law which bans the burial of animals in human cemeteries, in 1977 Hélène

Lavanent and Yvette Soltane booked themselves graves in a pet cemetery so that they could be buried with their dogs.

In 1984, a Texan hairdresser was upset when her pet Rottweiler killed and ate her four-week-old daughter, but mortified when she was told that the animal would have to be put down. She told newspaper reporters, 'I can always have another baby, but I can't replace my dog Byron.'

A Dutch veterinary surgeon's efforts to treat a sick cow literally backfired on him in 1977. He inserted a tube into the cow's anus to sample the cow's stomach gases, and thoughtlessly struck a match: a sudden burst of methane produced a jet of flame which set fire to the whole farm causing over £40,000 of damage. The cow however escaped unscathed.

In case of nuclear attack, don't forget to duck

During the cold war of the 1950s, many American civil defence 'experts' got rich from the booming trade in books giving advice on how to survive a nuclear war. One of the best sellers was David Watson's *Atomic Bombing: How To Protect Yourself*, which reassured readers that as American skyscrapers were built on heavy steel frames they 'would withstand the blast of an atomic bomb', and advised, 'steaks are a must in the diet of a burns patient', and 'curl up in a ball as you hit the ground'.

No one is quite sure why, but the English language uses the sex act as a basis for its lexicon of swear words more than any other. In Germany most swearing is profoundly anal: nearly every German joke there is to be told leads inexorably to a punchline containing the lynchpin expletive *Scheiss* (shit), *Dreck* (crap) or *leck mich im Arsch* (lick my arse). Scatological themes pepper the whole of German culture, resulting in a German sense of humour which can appear to be very ponderous and lacking in subtlety. Italian sufferers of Tourette's Syndrome – a condition which causes compulsive swearing – have a massive vocabulary of profanities to choose from, most of them based around religious themes, and usually referring to God and the Virgin Mary. Most lose a little in translation, especially *porco Dio* (that pig of a God), the confusing *Dio cane* (that dog of a God) or *Dio serpente* (that snake of a God), the very odd *Dio canarino* (that canary of a God) and *Dio scapa da letto senza scarpi* (God escaped from bed without shoes). Mussolini once launched a campaign to try to persuade his people to be a little less foul-mouthed, and a series of notices appeared all over the country ordering *Non bestemmiare per l'onore dell'Italia* (do not swear for the honour of Italy). All that these notices did, however, was encourage people to invent a new crop of oaths directed at *Il Duce* and his ****ing notices. The Spaniards are skilled and enthusiastic swearers, their oaths tending towards long-winded anal references, as in the popular *cago en la leche de tu madre* (I shit on your mother's milk), or ingenious combinations of religion and scatology, as in *me cago en Dios* (I shit on God) and *me cago en todos los santos* (I shit on all the saints), an invitation to a triple-whammy thunderbolt if ever there was one. The all time Spanish no. 1 oath, however, is still the multi-purpose *caramba*, which doesn't appear to have any meaning at all.

The Greek billionaire Aristotle Onassis had a bar stool on his yacht which was upholstered with the skin of a whale's penis. One day the American actress Betsy Drake, who was once married to Cary Grant, was sitting on the very stool when someone related this interesting item of trivia to her. 'Oh my God,' she shrieked as she leaped off it, 'Moby's dick!'

Food For Thought

Ghastronomy

Fruit Bat Soup[1]
Earthworm Broth[2]
Hedgehog Soup[1]
Scaly Anteater Soup[1]
Cobra Soup[1]

* * *

Stewed Rook[3]
Fried, Roasted or Boiled Guinea Pig[6]

* * *

Boiled Bamboo Rat[2]
Deep Fried Grasshopper[2]
Deep Fried Wasps[1]
Deep Fried Gecko[4]

* * *

Horse-Dung with Mustard and Cress Salad[3]

* * *

Crispy Fried Rat with Lemon[5]

* * *

Gecko Blood Liqueur[4]

[1] Thailand. [2] China. [3] British, eighteenth-century. [4] Vietnam.
[5] Canton. [6] Ecuador.

The durian fruit, considered a delicacy in parts of Asia, has a fragrance identical to that of a rotting corpse.

Ursula Beckley of Long Island, USA, filed a $3.6 million suit for damages against a local supermarket in 1989 after the three-egg omelette she was making suddenly yielded an unexpected protein bonus in the form of a healthy, six-inch black snake. Her lawyers said that she had been so deeply traumatised that it was unlikely she would be able to look at an egg ever again.

The legal definition of '100 per cent beef' includes heart, kidney, liver, pancreas, tail, thymus and head meat, comprising snout, lip, tongue and other muscle or fatty tissue. Until 1989 the animal's central nervous system, including the brain, was routinely used in the manufacture of burgers, meat pies, soups and stock cubes.

In parts of Malaysia cats are often killed by scalding, then their eyes are gouged out and eaten raw. They say it's very good for your eyesight.

Apart from in the comfort of your own home, the places most likely to cause you to die from food poisoning are restaurants or buffet receptions, followed by hospitals, institutions, schools and works canteens.

Every year 2,500 Americans choke to death on food. It is the sixth most common cause of death in the US.

'The custom of the sea' was the British navy's nineteenth-century euphemism for eating your shipmates – a legitimate and almost routine method of keeping alive when sailors were shipwrecked and starving. The order of priority on the menu was decided by the drawing of straws.

During the course of a lifetime you will consume about 13lb of dirt, most of it from unwashed vegetables.

Most British daily pintas arrive on the doorstep courtesy of a dairy cow which is being slowly milked to death. Dairy cows are only built to produce about five litres of milk a day, but intensive farming often forces them to yield five to eight times that amount. Although the cow should have a lifespan of about 30 years, she is physically broken and prematurely decrepit at the age of six or seven. By this time she is considered fit only for burger bar fodder: her head is thrown away and the rest of her goes into a giant crusher, to be mashed into a pink slurry.

Whilst dining, Fijian cannibals always saved their victims' brains as a treat for the ladies.

Northern lights
Tripe, once the diet of the poor in the north of England, is now only likely to be found on the menus of London's most fashionable restaurants, displayed as *tripes à la*

mode de Caen or *trippa alla Romana*. You will find brains listed on the same menus as *cervelles au beurre noir*.

Cat meat is served in Belgian restaurants as *lapin sans tête*, or 'headless rabbit'.

According to people who have tried it, there is absolutely no difference between the taste of cooked human flesh and pork. The Fijian language makes the point succinctly: the phrase for 'pig' is *puaka dina*; the phrase for 'human' is *puaka balava*, literally 'long pig'.

The main ingredient of the popular Chinese dish of bird's nest soup is saliva.

Factory-reared piglets are taken from their sows when they are two weeks old and spend the rest of their lives in a 'growing section', where boredom leads to aggression and often cannibalism against other pigs. When the pigs are moved to larger pens the shock often kills them.

Digestive biscuits were originally made in 1892 as an aid to control flatulence.

Meats starts to rot the moment the animal has been killed. The practice of hanging meat is done to allow the bacteria to break down the tissue and cellular walls: the more rotten and decomposed a piece of meat is, the more it will melt in your mouth.

One in every six pre-packed sandwiches sold over the counter could give you food poisoning.

Whenever you find a hole in a turnip, you may want to pause to consider the female turnip eelworm, which lives mostly inside the vegetable. You may wish to consider also the male of the species, which mates with her by poking his penis through a hole in the turnip skin.

Mean cuisine
To help them see better, Maoris ate the eyes of men they slew in battle.

The puffer fish, considered a great delicacy in Japan, is lethal if it is not cooked and prepared in precisely the right way, and no chef with less than three years' experience is allowed to serve it.

The botulism bacteria *Clostridium botulinum* can resist being boiled to temperatures of 212°F and produces a fatal toxin in conjunction with canned products. One ounce of the germ could theoretically kill one hundred million people.

Most scientists agree that the transference of BSE – 'mad cow disease' – to humans via infected meat is a possibility which cannot yet be ruled out, as the incubation period for the nearest human equivalent of BSE, Creutzfeldt-Jakob disease, is twelve years. Zoonoses – cross-infections between man and animal – are common: we already share 65 different diseases with dogs, 50 with cattle, 46 with sheep and goats, 42 with pigs, 35 with horses, 32 with rats and mice and 26 with poultry.

Chihuahuas were originally bred by the Chinese for their meat.

Life is what happens while you're busy making flans

The single biggest ever case of food poisoning occurred in Spain in 1981. Ramon and Elias Ferrero along with 36 other company executives were jailed for a combined total of 60,000 years when 600 people died after using their contaminated cooking oil.

The Ancient Romans deliberately added lead to their meals to make their food easier to digest.

Cases of reported food poisoning have increased fifteen-fold in the last ten years. 10,000 Britons suffer from food poisoning every week, and 100 people die from it every year.

In Regency London, the rich and fashionable ate lions' testicles for their alleged aphrodisiac properties.

When crops failed all over Europe in the early fourteenth century, troops were posted on gibbets in France and Germany to prevent people from rushing the gallows and cutting down and eating the corpses of hanged criminals. In England the famine was so great that horsemeat was considered a delicacy suitable only for noble tables. Most ordinary people ate dogs, cats and vermin.

A 'good' English butcher, while slitting the throat of a pig, would make sure that it died slowly, because a lengthy bleeding time improved the flavour of the meat. It was also common practice for butchers to whip sheep and pigs to death because it was supposed to make the meat more tender.

The parasite *Cryptosporidium*, which can cause severe diarrhoea, occurs naturally in British tap water. About 10,000 cases are reported every year, including about 2,000 which require hospital treatment.

Ephestia elutella, more commonly known as the cocoa moth, lives in chocolate. It reaches the chocolate factory hidden in the raw materials and lays eggs in the finished goods, which in turn produce worms.

Don't try this at home if you're on a diet, but a recipe once favoured by Indian princes involved the following: take one whole camel, and put a goat inside it. Stuff the goat with a peacock, which in turn should be stuffed with a chicken. Stuff the chicken with a sand grouse, the sand grouse with a quail, and the quail with a sparrow. Put the camel in a hole in the ground and steam.

In Iraq it is illegal to eat snakes on a Sunday.

Factory-reared animals are often unwittingly forced into cannibalism because their feed contains bone meal from rendered offal. They are also fed raw manure mixed into their food. Until there was a public outcry in 1990 following the death of a cat from a condition related to 'mad cow disease', pet food manufacturers regularly recycled brain tissue, chicken excrement, soiled straw, feathers and the remains of dead birds for tinned dog and cat food and dog and cat biscuits. There is no guarantee that the practice has now stopped completely, but pet food manufacturers point out that you are still more likely to find lean meat in a tin of dog food than you are in a pork pie.

In 1991, a restaurant owner in China was jailed for serving his customers dumplings stuffed with human flesh. The delicacy, listed on the menu at Wang Guang's White Temple Restaurant as heavily spiced Sichuan-style dumplings, had become a firm favourite with his regulars over a period of about four years. The fillings were supplied by Guang's brother, a crematorium assistant, who thought he had hit on a profitable sideline by taking his work home with him. The ruse was discovered when the parents of a young woman who had died in a road accident discovered that their daughter's body was incomplete when they came to cremate her.

Spiders on bread and butter is a traditional Kentucky cure for constipation.

One of Chicago's leading butchers of the 1870s, German-born Adolph Luetgert, achieved his lifelong ambition to become America's best-known sausage maker. When Luetgert was tried for the murder of his wife Louisa it was revealed that he'd melted her down in one of his giant vats and incorporated her into his sausage production line. After his conviction, public enthusiasm for sausages dwindled to the point where virtually none were sold in Illinois or neighbouring Michigan for almost two years.

Tomato ketchup was first sold in the US in 1830 as a patent medicine.

Flied lice

The Chinese diet could soon include maggots from the common house fly. Scientists at Beijing's Agricultural University have developed a high-nutrition, low-fat maggot and are currently negotiating with food and pharmaceutical firms to put them into mass production. Evidently, just 35 oz of maggots produce 17.5 oz of pure protein and 7 oz of low-fat oil and amino acids, and one fly can produce millions of maggots every week – the ideal convenience snack when you've got 1.2 billion mouths to feed.

In the Middle Ages, an outbreak of mass hysteria known as 'dancing mania' which reportedly caused men and women to dance around screaming and begging to be freed from demons inside them, was probably caused by food poisoning. A mould called ergot would often infect bread made from rye, and contained small amounts of LSD, which in turn caused hallucinations. A similar outbreak of ergot poisoning took place in France in 1951.

The Chinese regard the meat of the black chow as an aphrodisiac.

In 1835, two young Frenchmen enjoyed an expensive meal in one of Paris's finest restaurants. When they were presented with the bill they admitted frankly that they had no money and no intention of paying up. When the restaurant proprietor threatened them with the police, they laughed and told him he would be wasting his time because they had taken arsenic with their brandies. The following day, when a debt collector hired by the restaurateur arrived at their lodgings, he found them both dead.

In August 1983, the *Times* reported that a man living in West Germany had found a human finger in his bread finger roll.

Eighteen with a mullet

Channel 4's tabloid TV show *The Word* put to the test a cynical hypothesis that some of their viewers were dumb enough to do just about anything to get themselves on British television, even if only for about 45 seconds. It was a theory which proved to be depressingly accurate. In spite of an increasingly nauseating range of gastronomic tasks devised by the show's production team, there was no shortage of desperate types willing to humiliate themselves for fleeting glory. The 1993–4 run ended with a teenager unwisely attempting mouth to mouth on a dead fish before solemnly intoning to camera, 'I'd do anything to get on TV'. Earlier in the series, more vivid palate-tickling highlights included the moment the camera zoomed in on the bloodless face of a girl who had just popped a live garden slug into her mouth, the student who was filmed eating a quarter of a pound of lard, several who failed in the attempt to eat raw sheep's testicles, and another who ate from a bowl of breakfast cereal liberally laced with human verrucas, corns and toenail clippings. The feature arguably reached an epicurean nadir on 4 February 1994 when viewers saw a 25-year-old named Chris tuck into a garden worm buttie.

Have a Nice Death

Whitney Houston is Top of the Pops in Britain's crematoria. The most requested tune at services is *I Will Always Love You* from the film *The Bodyguard*.

Funerals in the US are a lot more sanitised than their European equivalents, because Americans avoid what they consider to be the unnecessarily distressing aspects of death. This process has been taken to its logical conclusion in California, where it is increasingly common for even the corpse to be excluded from the funeral.

On 16 October 1793, 200,000 people turned out to watch Marie Antoinette lose her head. They were all kept waiting while the executioner Sanson untied her hands so she could empty her bowels in a corner behind a wall.

A born-again Christian from Texas, Judge Charles J. Hearn, likes to demonstrate his new-found faith by adding a smiley face to his signature. Some of his critics have pointed out that this is not very appropriate behaviour for a judge, especially a judge signing a death warrant. The defence lawyer for a man sentenced to death by Judge Hearn in 1993 complained, 'It's like he's saying "have a nice death".'

In Belgium, buried corpses are dug up after a few years so that someone else can use the grave.

The famous US sports personality Phil Rizzuto was broadcasting a live Yankee baseball game when he was informed that Pope Paul VI had just died. 'Well,' said Rizzuto on air, 'that kind of puts the damper on even a Yankee win.'

Owing to bad planning when William the Conqueror died in 1087, his marble coffin was found to be far too small for the late King to fit inside it. Two soldiers were asked to stand on the body to squeeze it in, which they did with considerable enthusiasm, jumping up and down until they broke the King's back. The broken spine tore a hole in his stomach and caused it to explode with a terrible bang – the stench was so appalling that everyone had to run out of the building. In later years thieves broke into the coffin twice and stole every last bit of him except his left femur.

In Naples, corpses are stored in lockers and taken out and examined every now and then.

Most Russians will only stand in line for hours for

something edible, but Vladimir Ilyich Lenin continues to be a crowd-puller in his new mausoleum in St Petersburg, even though neither his reputation nor the queues are quite what they used to be. Under his blue acrylic tailored three-piece suit, the father of Communism also wears a rubber wetsuit into which is poured the solution which keeps him from falling apart. About 60 per cent of his body is now made of wax, including his ears: the original pickling in 1924 wasn't done properly and bits of him have since gone off. He also sports a growth of fungus around his neck and the back of his head which certainly wasn't there when he led the Bolsheviks to power in 1917. When Communism was still popular, Lenin had to be refrigerated with equipment from a German fish freezing plant to stop him melting from the body heat of visiting tourists. All this, after he had specifically asked in his will for a simple burial in accordance with his egalitarian principles.

Arnold Bennett's novels were renowned for their remarkable attention to detail. He was once complimented on his description of the death of Darius Clayhanger in the *Clayhanger* series, one of the most realistic death scenes in English literature. It was a doddle, explained Bennett. 'All the time my father was dying I was at the bedside making copious notes.'

The Jivaro people of South America bury their women and children under their floorboards. The men, however, are placed in a sitting position in a hut, then the corpse and the hut are set ablaze.

The Black Death was so called because victims turned black after bleeding into their skin. There were three main types of plague, of which the two most frequently occurring were pneumonic, the swift death breathed from person to person, and bubonic, which resulted in festering, stinking buboes, when the lymph glands in the groin and armpits became swollen like rotten peaches. Plague victims in London were often mugged by the nurses sent out to care for them. Some of the more impatient nurses strangled their victims or would rub infected pus into healthy people to ensure another pay day. The physician Nathaniel Hodges described how a greedy nurse hovered around an infected household until the whole family was dead, then systematically stripped them of their belongings, only to drop dead herself on the street outside, loaded with loot.

Some native South Americans ate the bodies of their deceased parents, but regarded cremation as a revolting sacrilege.

When Queen Mary attended the funeral of her brother

Adolphus, who died in 1927, neither she nor the rest of the mourners could have failed to hear her brother's body explode noisily inside his coffin during the funeral procession.

Masai tribesmen leave their deceased relatives out in the open for the hyenas to feed on.

When the united Italy's first ever monarch King Victor Emmanuel II died, Rome's daily paper *Opinione* wrote a 'live' eye-witness report on the state of their freshly deceased king: 'He lies with his face turned slightly to the left. His eyes are closed and his appearance, maintaining a certain look of pride, has taken on an aspect of calm which is enhanced by his natural pallidness. At 7 p.m. this evening, the embalming of the royal corpse will begin.' *Opinione* went on to assure readers that the embalming process would guarantee that 'the mortal remains of the appearance of our beloved sovereign will be conserved for the benefit of prosperity.' This confidence was sadly misplaced; the old King's natural pallidness turned rapidly into a very natural smell as he quickly decomposed in his new general's uniform, forcing attendants to flee with handkerchiefs covering their noses.

Esprit de corpse
The Cocoma tribe of Peru used to imbibe the ground-up bones of their relatives in fermented drinks, on the

basis that it was better to be inside a warm friend than out there in the cold earth.

When King Francis I of Naples died aged 52, custom decreed that the royal corpse lie in state in an elaborate cask for three days. On the third night, the two sentries on duty beside him were startled by a thud. They had a quick peek inside the cask then ran screaming into the night. Apparently one of the King's arms had dropped off.

Some Australian Aboriginal tribesmen traditionally lacerated themselves at funerals as a mark of respect for the dead, while widows would burn their breasts, arms and legs with firebrands. Occasionally things got so completely out of hand that the mourning would add to the death toll.

In 1994, researchers at Ohio State University discovered that bereavement is bad for your health.

In the 1980s, a group of Filipino vigilantes took to digging up corpses from graveyards and stealing kneecaps, which they wore around their necks to protect them from bullets.

Under cover of darkness, on the evening of 22 October 1928, the remains of eight unidentified members of the royal family were quietly removed from the royal vault of St George's Chapel, Windsor and reinterred at Frogmore. It was rumoured that the coffins were considered a liability after one of them had exploded during Evensong.

In rural Greece, the women of the family are required to dig up the bones of their deceased after five years have elapsed and examine them to see if they are clean enough to be placed in the communal ossuary.

Because of a fault in the embalming process, the body of Chairman Mao is shrinking at a steady rate of about five per cent a year. The official line given by the mausoleum director, however, is that this is merely an optical illusion caused by the curious lighting effects in the hall which contains his corpse.

Cremation is a very difficult business even with modern furnaces, which is why crematoria have electrically operated machines designed to grind up unburnt bones.

Whenever an Indonesian Mambai tribesman died, it was customary for the corpse to be seated in the family

112

house while relatives sat around and watched it rot for as long as they could tolerate the stench. In some parts of Indonesia, on the death of a husband his widow was obliged to rub fluids from his decomposing corpse into her skin.

The ritual governing the French Court at Versailles was as strict in death as it was in life. Within minutes of the expiration of a member of the French royal family, the royal bedroom would turn into a crowded abattoir, as six or seven physicians performed an on-the-spot autopsy before an audience of lords and ladies-in-waiting. The body was slowly cut to pieces, the head sawn open and examined and the royal entrails placed on silver salvers. The doctors would then make notes and pronounce their verdict on the cause of death. The death of King Louis XV was an exceptionally traumatic experience even by Versailles standards. A handful of courtiers, bound by their official duties, were forced to remain on duty in the infected sick room despite the terrible stench given off by the suppurating pustules on the King's body, which was itself already beginning to decay at an alarming rate. The corpse had quickly reached such a state of putrescence that the doctors didn't dare embalm him. Labourers had to be forcibly commandeered to place the body in a lead coffin, which was filled with quicklime, camphorated spirit and aromatic herbs, and quickly sealed. Even then the smell was so overpowering that those escorting the hearse had to cover their faces. The King's rotting remains were said to have been so horrible that one of the workmen paid to place them in the box is said to have died from a fit of uncontrollable vomiting.

Whenever a King of Thailand died, his body would be stored in a large golden urn in the palace for 100 days, during which time food would be placed before it daily at his regular mealtimes.

Australian Aboriginals in Queensland used to remove the kneecaps of their dead to prevent them returning from the grave.

(I Can't Get No) Putrefaction

When the Stevenage grocer Henry Trigg died in 1724, he left curious instructions in his determination to keep the hands of bodysnatchers away from his corpse. His coffin was placed in the rafters of his barn, where it remained on view for almost 250 years while the premises changed hands, to be used first as an inn, and later a bank. When the coffin was finally taken down and opened it was found to be empty. It seems the 'resurrection men' may have got to him after all.

In Fiji it was once traditional for bereaved wives to be strangled or buried alive with their deceased husbands. A similar custom prevailed in New Guinea, whereby the widow would request strangulation so that she could accompany her husband on his passage to the next world.

British undertakers got themselves a bad name in the eighteenth and nineteenth centuries because of their antisocial practice of mounting a watch on the door of a seriously ill person in anticipation of a new customer.

Return to Cinder

The Tomb of Mausolus, one of the Seven Wonders of the World which was later completely destroyed by an earthquake, was built in 353 BC in Turkey by Queen Artemisia on the death of her husband King Mausolus. The original idea was that the King's body was to be placed in the tomb, but there was a last minute change of plan: the Queen had him cremated, then poured his ashes into a goblet of wine and drank the lot.

In Irian Jaya, Indonesia, deceased leaders and persons of great power were slowly smoked over a fire for several months then hung from the eaves of their houses. From this position they could keep a benevolent eye on the family home for possibly hundreds of years.

The world's first exclusively gay funeral parlour was opened in San Francisco in February 1984.

The skull of Pope Clement VI, who died in 1352, was later used by the Huguenots as a football.

The dramatist Ben Jonson asked his patron King Charles I a personal favour: he requested a square foot of his own in Westminster Abbey where he could be buried when he died. The King agreed, and stuck to his word. Jonson got exactly one square foot, and had to be buried upright in it.

In many cultures the funeral is an opportunity to celebrate joyously the life of the deceased, not to mourn their death. The most extreme example of this is practised by the Nyakyusa people of Africa, where younger tribesmen and women sometimes copulate at the graveside.

The condition of British churchyards in the nineteenth century was so bad that grave robbing was a relatively easy business. Until the smell became too bad, it was very rare for bodies to be buried more than just two or three inches deep because of obstruction by bones and old coffins. Mourners would often find themselves stepping on the partly decomposed bodies of earlier internees. Dickens remarked that the predominant smell in London's churches was 'rot and mildew and dead citizens'. The cholera epidemics of the nineteenth century were blamed by some on urban churchyards, because matter from decomposing bodies could easily seep into wells and streams. The black flies which frequently emerged from coffins and infested the chapels were known to Sunday school children as 'body bugs'.

James I tried to kick-start the British wool trade by making it compulsory for everyone to be buried in a pure woollen shroud. The law wasn't repealed until 1814.

In Southeastern Australia, if a young Aboriginal mother died, her live infant would be placed in the grave and buried with her.

Queen 'Bloody' Mary's widowed husband, King Philip of Spain, literally rotted to death. In 1598 a huge tumour appeared on his thigh and he fell ill with a fever. The court surgeon lanced it, but infection spread and soon the King's entire body was covered with huge, festering boils. He lay in bed in agony, allowing no one near enough either to touch him, change his bandages or even place a bedpan under him, and so the King lay for days in his own excreta. The stench from his body became so bad that the poor maids who spoon-fed him had to cover their mouths with handkerchiefs, but the cowardly court doctors still refused to allow his servants to move him or change his bedclothes. Soon maggots began to appear in the King's open sores, but when his doctors tried to clean the vermin out he screamed in pain and they retreated again. Eventually the King's body began to putrefy, and when he became too weak to put up an argument the physicians moved in and tried to clean him up by applying live leeches to the wounds. The rotting process was so awful that an eye-witness said that 'all that could be seen of His Majesty . . . were his eyes and his tongue.' After nearly eight weeks of this Philip died, aged 71.

When Enrico Caruso died in 1921, the great Italian opera singer was put on show in a glass coffin, allowing his hordes of fans to ogle his corpse. Five years and several new suits later, his widow decided to give him a more dignified interment in a private tomb.

The last word in picture postcards is sold by the Sisters of the Convent of Capuccini in Palermo, Sicily. Instead of the more traditional landscape shots, the nuns have opted for photographs of their convent walls, which have been decorated for generations with cadavers, strung up fully dressed in their street clothes. Their convent is now one of Palermo's biggest tourist attractions.

When Albert Einstein died in 1955, his body was cremated while his brain was preserved in a glass jar. Rather conceitedly it was Albert's dying wish that his best bit should be saved in case *post mortem* analysis shed new light on the rare gift of human genius. It didn't.

To protect the newly buried from the 'resurrection men', Britain's graves were often booby trapped or manned by armed guards. Medical students searching for corpses to dig up were often badly injured by spring guns or trip wires. Even more drastic measures were taken by a bereaved parent from Edinburgh who had a landmine placed on his daughter's grave. One of the most effective deterrents was to have a one ton slab of granite lowered on to the grave with a block and tackle. In Yorkshire a so-called 'Resurrection Stone' was hired out to the bereaved at a guinea a fortnight. Another popular security device was the iron mortsafe – a heavy iron grille which formed a cage around the coffin. As soon as the body was sufficiently decomposed for the danger to have passed, it was loaned to the next customer.

The Persian King Cambyses II had a finely tuned sense of poetic justice. When one of his judges was found guilty of corruption, Cambyses had him flayed, then had the judge's old seat reupholstered with his skin. Then he appointed the dead judge's son to sit in judgment where his father had previously sat.

The hands of the Argentinian President General Juan Perón were cut off in 1987 and ransomed for £5 million. Fortunately Perón had no further use for them as he had already been dead for thirteen years.

Old stiff-in-the-mud
'Lindow Man', an Iron Age corpse recovered from a peat bog in the north of England, was dubbed Pete Marsh by the press when it was found in 1986. Peat bogs offer excellent opportunities for preserving human tissue, as a local man discovered to his eternal regret. When a woman's head was found in the same bog a few months earlier he walked into the nearest police station and confessed to the murder of his wife. By the time experts had confirmed that the leathery relic had been lying there since AD 200, it was a bit too late for him to change his mind.

The Berawan tribe of Borneo store their dead relatives in large earthenware jars, and as the corpse rots, bodily fluids are drained off through a hole in the bottom via a bamboo tube. Later the dried remains are removed and interred in a smaller receptacle. The big jars are too valuable to waste on a body because they can also be used in the kitchen to make rice wine.

A couple of dinner guests of the deranged Roman Emperor Elagabalus one day complimented him on the flower arrangement which adorned the imperial table, carelessly conjecturing how pleasant it would be to be smothered in the scent of roses. The Emperor was a very obliging sort of chap: the next time they sat at his table he had them suffocated to death under several tons of petals.

Marriages Made in Heaven

Louis XIV's 75-year-old second wife Madame de Maintenon confessed to her priest that she found the effort of having sex with the 70-year-old King twice every day rather tiring.

When King Ferdinand I of Naples was asked on the morning after his wedding night how he liked his new bride Maria, he replied, 'She sleeps like the dead and sweats like a pig.'

Before he married her mother, Queen Victoria's father lived openly for 27 years with a retired French-Canadian prostitute.

Elizabeth, the wife of the poet and painter Rossetti, died in 1862 after accidentally overdosing on laudanum she was taking for her neuralgia. Rossetti, himself an alcoholic and morphine addict, was so grief stricken that as a token of his love he had a pile of his unpublished manuscripts wrapped in her golden hair and buried with her in her coffin. Seven years later, however, he had a change of heart and decided he wanted them back. Up came Elizabeth, and the poems were dusted off and published to great critical acclaim.

The Emperor Nero was besotted with his beautiful second wife Poppaea, and once wrote a song about her fabulous long auburn hair. Three years after the wedding day, however, while Poppaea was pregnant, they had a tiff during which Nero accidentally kicked her to death. The Emperor was grief-stricken, but found consolation soon afterwards when he spotted a young male slave named Sporus who very much resembled the late Mrs Nero. The Emperor had him castrated and together they went through a marriage ceremony.

The author and critic John Ruskin found the sight of his wife's pubic hair on their wedding night so shocking that he never slept with her again.

Although Charles Darwin was the first person to elucidate the dangers of inbreeding, he wasn't quite bright enough to avoid marrying his own first cousin Emma. There were signs of eccentricity on both sides of the family, which was already dangerously interlinked. His grandmother and great-grandfather were unstable drunks, his uncle Erasmus was insane and committed suicide, and his brother Erasmus was a chronic and neurotic invalid. His grandfather, yet another Erasmus, who had a terrible stammer, was considered a leading expert on the treatment of the mentally ill. He had whirling beds and gyrating chairs fitted into most of the country's lunatic asylums so that patients could be rotated until blood poured out of their ears, eyes and noses. Charles Darwin himself was also a stammerer and a morose hypochondriac; he suffered from fainting fits and would take to his bed for months at a time.

Give or take half a dozen, the Polish King Augustus II 'The Strong' fathered 365 bastards. It didn't go down very well with his wife Eberdine, who was so embarrassed by his behaviour that she hardly ever set foot in Poland throughout her husband's rein.

On 11 June 1831, Moses Alexander, aged 93, was married to Frances Tompkins, aged 105, in New York. The following morning the newlyweds were both taken dead from their bed.

Alexis Mikhailovich, the second ruler of the House of Romanov, was regarded as one of the more laid back and tolerant Czars because he only had about 7,000 of his subjects tortured and executed throughout his entire reign. When his first wife Mary died he decided to marry again, and chose his new bride according to the Russian tradition of *smotrinya*. His country's most beautiful maidens were summoned to the Kremlin and subjected to intimate internal and external examination, which was a cross between a Miss Russia pageant and a customs body search. Girls who didn't pass muster were unceremoniously dumped outside the Kremlin gates. Eventually the Czarina's job was given to one Natalya Naryshkina: in return she gave him Peter the Great, his fourteenth child. As Peter stuck out like a sore thumb because he was the only normal infant in a nursery full of deformed or imbecile children, it is likely that Czar Alexis wasn't the real father.

In rural Turkey, it is still customary for a mother-in-law to give her son's prospective bride a body search in a public baths before she will consent to the marriage.

His wife Catherine the Great may have been one of history's biggest nymphomaniacs, but Czar Peter III spent his entire honeymoon and most of his married life playing with toy soldiers under the bedsheets.

Louis XV introduced himself to his new Polish wife Maria by making love to her seven times on their wedding night. He was fifteen years old at the time.

Waiting for the kids to die
The oldest couple ever to be divorced were Simon and Ida Stern, who parted company in Milwaukee, USA in February 1984. He was 97, she was six years younger.

Although the King's brother Philippe, the Duke of Orléans, was one of history's most famous homosexuals, French court etiquette required that he had to have a full time, fully paid official court mistress. Madame de Grancey was never actually allowed in his bedroom and was quite happy to spend all of her time playing cards. Although Philippe's second wife stood at least eighteen inches taller than him, was considerably more butch than he was, and frightened the living daylights out of him, the couple were able – for dynastical purposes only – to produce three children. Philippe revealed afterwards that this had only been possible because he had on each occasion rubbed his penis with a holy medal for luck.

Until about one hundred years ago, it was common for wealthy Egyptian men on their wedding night to pay a servant to consummate the marriage for them, proof of the old Arab saying, 'A woman for duty, a boy for pleasure, but a melon for ecstasy.'

Although Peter the Great had long since ditched his first wife Eudoxia and remarried, he was stricken by understandable pangs of jealousy when he found that his ex had a new man in her life. The following day at precisely 3 p.m. the Czar had a wooden stake driven up her lover's rectum.

When England's King John found that his wife Isabella had taken a lover, he had him killed and his corpse strung up over Isabella's side of the bed.

Under sixteenth-century English law, men could only beat their wives before 10 p.m.

The first Hanoverian to ascend the British throne, George I, divorced his wife then had her locked up in a German castle for 32 years. His particularly vindictive approach to separation was probably because she had infected him with syphilis and he wanted revenge.

In Java, married farmers sometimes copulate in their fields to make the soil more fertile.

George IV nearly fainted when he first clapped eyes on his wife, Caroline of Brunswick-Wolfenbüttel, so obese, ugly and sweaty was she. After sleeping together once on their wedding night, the couple went their own separate ways, never attempting to disguise the mutual loathing they felt for each other. When Napoleon Bonaparte died in 1821, a messenger rushed to inform the king, 'Your Majesty, your greatest enemy is dead.' George replied, 'Is she, by God?'

Catherine de Medici drilled a hole in her bedroom floor so she could watch her husband copulating with his mistress in the room below.

King George I introduced himself to his prospective new daughter-in-law, Princess Caroline of Ansbach, by lifting her skirts to see for himself whether or not his son was marrying a virgin.

Vera Czermak decided to take her own life when she found out that her husband had been unfaithful to her, and leaped from a third-floor window. She came to later in a hospital bed unable to understand why she wasn't dead. Doctors explained that the now late Mr Czermak had broken her fall.

Germany's Kaiser Wilhelm I and his wife Augusta rowed virtually every day of their married lives, which lasted nearly 60 years. When Wilhelm first became Emperor he couldn't be bothered to tell her about it: she heard the news from one of his footmen.

Many Victorian couples abstained from marital relations on Sundays because sex on the Sabbath was considered improper. Although Queen Victoria valued a healthy sex life, her husband Albert wasn't a keen collaborator on any day of the week. He always went to bed wearing a little all-in-one woollen sleeping suit, and once said of heterosexual intercourse, 'That particular species of vice disgusts me.'

The greatest age difference between a married couple

is 88 years. In 1983, a sixteen-year-old Bangladeshi girl, Marium Begun, became the fifth wife of 104-year-old Amin Ali Azam.

The Spanish Queen Juana 'The Mad' was unhinged to begin with, but was driven completely round the bend by her faithless and mostly absent husband Philip. When her beloved Philip died, aged 28, she resolved to see more of him in future. She had his body embalmed and kept it by her side at all times, even at mealtimes and in bed at night.

Leopold II, King of the Belgians took his second wife – a sixteen-year-old prostitute he'd discovered in a Paris brothel – when he was 74 years old. When the ceremony was over, he turned to one of the witnesses and said, 'Let me introduce you to my widow.' Three days later the King was dead.

Ever fallen in love with someone you shouldn't have fallen in love with?

Ivan the Terrible married eight times. His first three wives died young, the third, Martha, before the marriage was even properly consummated. Her demise, according to one account, was brought on by Ivan's excessively enthusiastic foreplay. He quickly became tired of his fourth wife, Anna, and had her packed off to a convent. The fifth Czarina, another Anna, was soon replaced by a sixth, Vasilissa, but when he discovered that she was seeing another man, Ivan had her lover impaled beneath her bedroom window. He found out that his seventh wife Maria had lied to him about her virginity when he married her, and promptly had her drowned the following day. His eighth and final wife Maria survived him. He died playing chess.

In 1994, a woman from Los Angeles took her husband to court in an attempt to force him to have an operation to reduce the size of his penis.

Mrs Dodie Wyanette waited hand and foot on her blind husband Harmon for eighteen years at their home in Miami, Florida, until his eyesight was restored by an operation in 1994. He then threw her out of the house because she was too ugly. 'She was a great wife as long as I didn't have to look at her,' explained husband Harmon. 'I never realised what a dog she was.'

Dirtysomething

In 1983, the Princess of Wales went on a walkabout in South Australia, mingling freely with the crowds of people who had turned out to see her and her husband Charles on their royal tour. Along the way she met a small boy and playfully tousled his hair.

'Why aren't you at school today?' Diana beamed.

'I was sent home,' replied the boy, 'because I've got head lice.'

In rural Ethiopia it is still the norm to bathe in the warm, running stream of a urinating cow.

Personal hygiene was considered such a novelty right up until the eighteenth century that public baths had a bad reputation. People who habitually bathed were regarded as ill, or sexual perverts, or both. So notorious were the 'stews' or public baths of late medieval Europe, that 'stew' came to be used as another word for brothel. Henry VIII shut down Britain's public baths in 1546 in an attempt to avert a syphilis epidemic.

Unusually for the time, the French King Henri IV

was renowned as a stickler for changing his shirts regularly: however, he still went around 'smelling like a carrion'. When his fiancée Marie de Médicis met him for the first time, the stench almost made her faint.

Children on the island of Tonga used to catch and eat their parents' head and body lice as a sign of filial duty and affection.

Filthy rich
The poor in seventeenth-century Britain rarely had more than one change of clothes, which made it all the more important that they washed once a week. The rich, however, who had large reserves of linen and could therefore keep going for months without washing, turned filthiness into a sign of affluence. Personal cleanliness became inversely proportional to your station in life: the higher up the social scale you were, the more you stank. At the very bottom were miners, who had to wash their pit-blackened clothes and bodies every single night.

Bathing indoors was considered a distinctly un-American activity well into the nineteenth century. When the White House had its first bathtub installed in 1851, it sparked a public uproar.

Body lice can carry many diseases, including plague. Native South Americans are prone to a plague-like infection of the tonsils thanks to their habit of cracking lice between their teeth.

Peter the Great and his entourage were renowned throughout Europe for their lack of personal hygiene, and were described as 'baptised bears'. Peter had a habit of walking on tables at mealtimes, and putting his feet in everyone's dishes. When the Czar and his courtiers visited London, onlookers noted that they dripped pearls and lice intermittently as they walked.

The average male foot exudes half a pint of sweat each day.

Even after soap was first produced commercially in England in 1824, most people were content to wash only their hands and face, seldom allowing soap or water near their armpits, feet or genitals for years on end.

Natives of Malabar who suffered from head lice would call for the local holy man, who would voluntarily take the lice and put them on his own head for nourishment.

As Frederick the Great grew older and more eccentric, he acquired a personal hygiene problem of epic proportions. His clothes remained unchanged for years and he shuffled in rags around his palace, which was ankle-deep in excrement produced by his pack of beloved Italian greyhounds. When he died, the shirt on his back was so rotten with sweat that his valet had to dress him in one of his own shirts for the burial.

In seventeenth-century France it was considered bad form to take lice, fleas or other parasites and crack them between one's fingernails in company 'except in the most intimate circles'.

Although Louis XIV was an enthusiastic lover, his advances must have been trying for those mistresses with keen olfactory awareness. When his doctor ordered him to bathe for medical reasons, the King got out of it by suddenly developing a terrible headache as soon as he had immersed himself in the water. He vowed never to repeat the experience again, although his doctors tried to coax him into having another bath twelve months later. This time Louis flatly refused.

A book of hygiene and manners published in 1671 advised children to avoid bathing wherever possible. 'Washing with water is bad for sight, causes toothache and catarrh, makes the face pale, and renders one more susceptible to cold in winter and sun in summer.'

Vive la différence

Some time during the sixteenth century, France became a nation of hydrophobics, who believed that water was a health hazard. The French held that human skin was permeable, and that hot water was especially dangerous because it opened the pores, exposing the inner body to dirty air. Water, they were told, also weakened internal organs and ligaments. Old habits die hard. Even today the French continue to harbour a suspicion that water is bad for the skin, which is why they take fewer baths and showers than almost anyone else in Europe. In a European league table of personal cleanliness, the Spanish come bottom, closely followed by the French, with the Italians, who take more baths and showers, and use more soap than anyone else, at the top. The average French adult uses 4.2 bars of soap a year – about half the amount consumed by the average Briton, and only one in every five French men takes a bath daily. The French, and the Spanish, are far more likely to spend money on perfumes to mask the smell of stale sweat. In Spain, even very small children are more likely to be doused with *eau de cologne* rather than be forced to bathe. The French also have the most casual attitude to dental hygiene in Europe: on average, they brush their teeth only once every three days. Although Scandinavians are now considered to be more conscientious about personal hygiene than most other nationalities, this hasn't always been so; a thousand years ago the Arab historian Ahmed ibn Fadlan described them as 'the filthiest race that God ever created. They do not wipe themselves after going to stool, nor wash themselves after a nocturnal pollution'.

In some Mediterranean communities, an infestation of lice is considered a sign of virility.

The US town of Montpelier in Vermont holds an

annual Rotten Sneakers Contest, the only one in the world. Previous competition winners include eight-year-old Robert Scruton, who prepared by refusing to take his world-beating Nikes off for two years beforehand.

The average speed at which a human breaks wind is about 96 miles per hour.

Osphresiology, the science of diagnosis by smell, was an eighteenth-century fad which briefly took the medical world by storm. Doctors claimed to be able to reach a diagnosis of the patient's ailment by smelling their sweat, stools and urine.

In accordance with the ancient Indian laws of Manu, any citizen who broke wind in front of the monarch was liable to have his posterior amputated.

A Little of What You Fancy

The 1897 Sears, Roebuck & Co. mail order catalogue offered a selection of hypodermic syringe kits for shooting up heroin.

According to the Old Testament, Noah was the first person ever to get pissed.

The Russian Empress Catherine I was constantly inebriated, and once even survived an assassination attempt too soused to realise that anything at all had happened. She was reviewing a Guards' regiment when a bullet flew past and struck an innocent bystander dead. The drunken Empress didn't react at all, and moved on.

The Danish King Frederick VII survived throughout his entire life on pea soup and bacon washed down with vast quantities of lager.

Every day for eighteen years the elusive and probably late Lord Lucan ate grilled lamb cutlets for lunch.

One of the most famous drunks in British history was the eleventh Duke of Norfolk, who enjoyed a debauched lifestyle in Regency London. The 'Dirty Duke' was alleged to have such an astonishing capacity for alcohol that he could drink five or six times more than any other man – even the Prince Regent himself, who was no slouch when it came to knocking back the odd gallon of cherry brandy. He and his friend the Prince were often seen together staggering around the streets of London blind drunk. When Norfolk was an old man, the Prince and his brothers thought it would be a good wheeze to get Norfolk to drink himself to death. They invited him to a drinking party and spiked his tumblers of wine with neat brandy; although his alcohol intake was about ten times more than he had intended, the Duke survived. He was also a disgusting glutton who in old age became so obese that he couldn't get through a standard door frame. He acquired his nickname because he never, ever washed. He complained one day to a friend, Dudley North, that he was crippled with rheumatism, and had tried everything to relieve the pain without effect. 'Pray, my Lord,' replied North, 'did you ever try a clean shirt?'

Ivan the Terrible was addicted to mercury, and always kept a cauldron of it by his bedside. Mercury was one of the only recognised cures for syphilis.

Queen Victoria ate too quickly, mixed whisky with her claret, and consequently was a martyr to her flatulence.

One of France's biggest debauchees ever was the Duke

of Orléans, regent to the boy-king Louis XV. He held orgies at his home most evenings, had naked prostitutes served up nightly to his dinner guests on silver salvers, and at one time kept 100 mistresses, every one of them renowned for their ugliness. When his mother chided him for his choice of women he replied, 'Mother, all cats are grey in the dark.' He allegedly slept with his favourite eldest daughter, the none too fragrant Duchess de Berry, who regularly drank herself senseless and would roll in her own vomit on the carpet until eventually, according to her death certificate, she ate herself to death. The Duke attained notoriety, however, for his drinking binges. He was already a senile and purple-faced old man in his early forties, although he was still capable of knocking back seven bottles of wine a night, and his friends marvelled that he was alive at all. When he arrived in London, people who had never seen him before placed bets that he would be dead within three months. In 1721, against the advice of his doctors, he took a new mistress who was nearly 30 years younger than him. The effect on his health was predictably disastrous: he was sitting by the fireplace of his drawing room at Versailles one day when he had a massive stroke. When a doctor tried to bleed him, a lady courtier shouted, 'No! You'll kill him . . . He has just lain with a whore.' Two hours later the Duke was dead, aged 49. Although everyone knew that the drink and wild living had killed him, royal etiquette required an official *post mortem*. Unfortunately, while it was being carried out, the Duke's favourite dog snatched up his master's heart and ate it.

Nearly half of all the middle-aged adults in North America suffer from clinical obesity.

In December 1993, a 47-stone Argentinian was rushed to hospital and placed on a respirator in the intensive care unit of a hospital in La Plata, near Buenos Aires, after eating a whole piglet for dinner.

The favourite tipple of not only the working classes but many writers and artists in nineteenth-century Paris was absinthe, a hallucinogenic liquor made from toxic wormwood oil. When it was drunk in large enough quantities, absinthe allegedly produced convulsions and brain damage, and was linked with a spate of murders and suicides.

No man is an island . . .

But Elvis came close. Apart from the kind of regular meals which would have made a Sumo wrestler blanch, including a supper which comprised three large cheeseburgers and six banana splits, he snacked for anything up to 24 hours per day. Towards the end of his life he binged compulsively on chocolate and ice-cream, and had a fridge installed in his bedroom filled with his favourite confectionery: Eskimo Pies and Nutty Buddys.

Louis XIV was a dedicated glutton, and like most of the Bourbons was a *gros bâtard*, or 'fat bastard'. Later in life, however, he struggled to force food through his pursed lips into his shrunken mouth. It had been that way ever since his doctors, while removing several of the King's bad teeth, had accidentally broken his upper jaw and smashed his palate. From that moment on

Louis had difficulty chewing, and bits of food often came down his nose. Louis XVI, who was also obese, ate so much chocolate that he appointed an official courtier at Versailles known as *Chocolatier* to the King.

Still queasy after all these years

Ernest Hemingway wrote all his works on a diet of peanut butter sandwiches.

Dr Johnson had a voracious appetite coupled with nauseating table manners. According to James Boswell, he swilled, gorged and stuffed himself until sweat ran down his cheeks and the veins stood out on his forehead. Johnson's favourite dish, which he took at the Cheshire Cheese inn off Fleet Street, was a vast pudding containing beefsteaks, kidneys, oysters, larks and mushrooms.

Socrates could drink and think you under the table at the same time. His ability to hold his liquor was legendary and he would continue to philosophise when everyone else at the banquet had long since passed out or gone home.

Between 1897 and 1914 the British royal family, which during that period was headed by Queen Victoria, Edward VII and George V respectively, was regularly supplied with cocaine and heroin. Record books from a pharmacy in Braemar show that while they were staying at Balmoral, the royals and their guests took delivery of cocaine and heroin solutions as well as sleeping pills. Heroin was considered non-addictive and was often used to wean people off opium.

The London 'gin epidemic' of the mid-eighteenth century – 'drunk for a penny, dead drunk for twopence' – had a practical side: gin was considered to be a much safer bet than water, and it had the added attraction of lowering one's sensitivity to bug bites.

Warning: smoking can seriously damage your health . . .

A Chinese decree of 1638 promised decapitation for anyone caught trafficking in tobacco.

Some Russian Czars deported smokers to Siberia, whilst others tortured them to death. The first Romanov Czar Mikhail Feodorovich ordered that offenders should have their nostrils slit.

Some of the most sought-after varieties of Virginia tobacco were arranged in bunches and left to cure in lavatories so that they would absorb the fumes of human ordure and urine.

A cigarette brand named Death, launched by a company in California, claims to be the first 'honest smoke'. Ten per cent of all its revenue is donated to cancer research, and the cigarette packs, which are branded with a skull and crossbones, bear a notice advising smokers to quit.

During the Plague, Eton schoolboys were made to smoke tobacco to ward off the disease.

When a Berewan tribesman of Borneo died, it was customary at the funeral to offer him a final fag. Either a lit cigarette would be placed in the corpse's mouth, or the wife and children of the deceased would take it in turns to lie beside the body smoking, occasionally offering the corpse a drag.

An estimated 40 per cent of all American NFL football players are regular users of cocaine, and 75 per cent use anabolic steroids. The known symptoms of steroid abuse include cardiovascular disease, salt retention and high blood pressure, furring of the arteries, chronic acne, liver and kidney damage and sterility.

Native Americans used cannabis resin to cure syphilis.

The last Czar of Russia Nicholas II spent the final two years of his reign high on a cocktail of addictive drugs. He took cocaine for colds, opium and morphine for stomach complaints, and hallucinogens, obtained from a herbalist. Visitors were shocked by his appearance and remarked on his dull eyes, dilated pupils, hollow cheeks, vacant smile and apparent lack of concern about the impending crisis.

Although alcoholism in Russia was a way of life, few could drink Peter the Great under the table. He was a huge man with a phenomenal capacity for alcohol. He created a drinking club known as his 'Synod of Fools and Jesters' as an excuse for regular drunken orgies. At the head of this company was the Kremlin's second biggest dipsomaniac, Nikita Zotov. Peter would pour vodka down the throats of his cronies with a funnel, while Zotov, seated on a high ceremonial chair, threw up on the heads down below. When the Czar's doctors begged him to take spa waters to repair some of the damage done to his body by alcohol he complied, as he also fancied himself as a bit of a medical man. He drank his cure, gulping down as many as twenty glasses of water one after the other, but always topped it up with alcohol to improve the flavour.

In 1818, the Maori chief Touai was shipped over to England from his native New Zealand and paraded around London's polite society for his curiosity value. The chief survived the culture shock surprisingly well and was able to live in London successfully for several years. Eventually, however, he became desperately homesick; he missed his family and his friends, but most of all he missed the taste of human flesh. Beef, he confessed to his hosts, he found a major bore. Where he came from the idea of a good Sunday roast involved the participation of a fleshy middle-aged man.

Europeans constitute just thirteen per cent of the world's population, but consume more than half the world's alcohol.

The Christmas tradition of flying reindeer has its origins in a rather less romantic Siberian ritual involving dangerous mind-altering substances. At feast times, the reindeer herdsmen would spike their drinks with an hallucinogen called fly agaric – a particularly potent drug similar to LSD which passes through the human digestive system relatively undiluted. When the herdsmen relieved themselves in the snow, their urine was lapped up by thirsty reindeer, who then also became high on the drug.

Heavy drinking, i.e. an alcohol intake of more than the 'safe' level of 21 units per week, shrinks your testicles.

The Bitterest Pill

Bayer, the company known for manufacturing aspirin, were the first people to use the word 'Heroin' as a brand name for their patent cough medicine. The exciting new wonder drug, first made in 1898 from synthesised morphine, was the subject of an intense advertising campaign at the turn of the century. Heroin was also used to 'cure' morphine addiction, to send babies with colic to sleep, and as a general painkiller. By 1920 the streets of New York City had far fewer hacking coughs, but an estimated 300,000 heroin addicts.

A popular seventeenth-century cure for toothache was sweat from the anus of a cat which had been chased across a ploughed field.

Statistically, doctors are very bad for your health: whenever they go on strike the death rate falls. During a strike by hospital doctors in Israel, hospital admissions fell by 85 per cent and the national death rate halved. When doctors in Bogota, Colombia downed tools for two months in 1976, the mortality rate dropped by 35 per cent. A similar strike in Los Angeles in the same year resulted in 60 per cent fewer admissions and an 18 per cent fall in the death rate. In every case as soon as the striking doctors went back to work, the death rate always returned to normal.

The finest collection of bladder stones ever assembled by one man was the work of the surgeon Sir Henry Thompson, urologist to the crowned heads of Europe. When Sir Henry died he bequeathed all 1000 of them, including a couple removed from Leopold I, King of the Belgians and France's Napoleon III, to the Royal College of Surgeons in London. The overwhelming temptation for medical students to have a game of 'shotties' with bits of two Emperors was removed in 1941 when the collection was destroyed by the blitz.

According to new research carried out at St Mark's Hospital, London, constipation can by cured by attaching electrodes to your anus.

If the official records of such events are to be taken seriously, royal patients are not only a lot braver than the rest of us, but also a great deal more courteous. After George IV had a sebaceous cyst removed from his head in 1821 entirely without the aid of anaesthetic, he casually enquired of the surgeon Astley Cooper, 'So, what do you call these tumours?' As a mark of the King's gratitude, plain Astley became Sir Astley.

147

Queen Victoria had a particularly nasty axillary abscess drained when she was 51 years old; when she came round from the chloroform she is supposed to have opened her eyes and remarked, 'A most unpleasant task, Professor Lister, most pleasantly performed.' The price of failure for a royal medic, however, has always been high, as demonstrated by Bohemia's blind King John. When surgeons failed to restore his sight he had the lot of them drowned in the Danube.

Ancient Egyptians cured toothache by splitting open the body of a live mouse, then laying it, still warm, along the patient's gums. Hippocrates highly recommended a toothpaste made from three mice and the head of a hare.

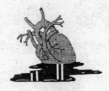

In 1822, the US Army surgeon William Beaumont treated a man named Alexis Martin for a gunshot wound in the abdomen which had left him with such a gaping hole that you could see right inside his stomach. Martin lived, but the wound refused to heal and the hole had to be plugged with wads of cloth to prevent the contents of his stomach from leaking out. He became a medical celebrity and allowed Beaumont to perform experiments on him for years afterwards.

For hundreds of years doctors listened to their patients' heartbeat by pressing an ear against the chest. In 1816 a doctor in Paris was confronted by a girl who had such enormous breasts that he could get nowhere near her without compromising the dignity of both parties. He cleverly rolled up a sheet of paper so that he could listen from a respectable distance, thus inventing the stethoscope.

Lord Dawson of Penn, the eminent royal physician who famously uttered the words: 'The King's life is drawing peacefully to its close,' before slipping a hypodermic full of morphine into George V's jugular, making sure his prose wasn't premature, served as royal doctor to four sovereigns: Edward VII, George V, Edward VIII and George VI. Although Lord Dawson was the best paid doctor in the country it didn't necessarily mean that he was the best man for the job. A rather vicious rumour went around that he once treated a patient for jaundice for six weeks until he realised that the man was Chinese.

In Ancient Rome about 5000 people a day died from measles, and it remained a major menace for hundreds of years. Measles is similar in many ways to smallpox, and doctors weren't able to distinguish between the two until the sixteenth century.

Doctors of the mad King of France Charles VI tried to cure him of his ills by sawing little holes in his skull to relieve pressure on his brain. When this didn't have much effect they attempted an early fifteenth-century version of shock treatment: ten men with blackened faces hid in his room, then leaped out at him. The King died, completely insane, seventeen years later.

An eighteenth-century cure for a nosebleed involved tying a frog around your neck.

Before the discovery of anaesthetics in the nineteenth century, patients undergoing surgery stood slightly more chance of dying from shock during treatment than they did from their original ailment.

Nineteenth-century doctors were confident that herpes was a sure sign of excellent health.

Catherine the Great tried to set an example when she became the very first person in Russia to receive the smallpox vaccine. It backfired, because her subjects were convinced she was mad and trying to commit suicide. The idea of infecting yourself with a deadly disease in order to protect yourself from the same disease seemed to be a sure sign of mental illness. Decades later, the Catholic Kings of Spain were still banning inoculation against smallpox on theological grounds, thus condemning generations of their own family to death in the process.

In the 1830s, doctors tried to cure consumption by handing out pills made from cobwebs.

In 1797, as the Prussian King Frederick William's bloated body lay worn out by a lifetime of debauchery, his court filled up with charlatans and quack physicians each hoping to make a quick profit out of the King's condition. He was told to inhale the breath of two new-born calves, to sleep between two children aged between eight and ten, and to listen to the sound of wind instruments, but in no circumstances to listen to violins. He tried them all and died from heart disease aged 53.

There was no recognised professional difference between a barber and a surgeon until 1745. Barbers were allowed to perform surgical operations simply because their scissors and razors made them obvious candidates for the job. They were bound by just one code of practice which banned them from either shaving or washing a man, or brushing his teeth on a Sunday. They were, however, free to blood-let, lance boils or excise tumours on any day they liked. In Henry V's army at Agincourt, surgeons and barbers squabbled on the battlefield over the right to perform amputations.

Although morphine is one of the most highly addictive drugs known to society – only 20–25 days' usage will produce a morphine junkie – it was used until the early twentieth century as a general painkiller for the most benign of ailments including colds and minor headaches. At the beginning of the 1900s, the US had over 3000 high-street stores selling over 50,000 different opium-based drugs over the counter. Morphine and opium were so widely used on the battlefield during the American Civil War – the former as a painkiller and the latter as a recreational drug – that opium addiction became known as the 'army disease'.

In the first century, Pliny recommended as a cure for halitosis 'pervasive green frogs, burnt heel of ox, toads and worms'. He also advised that mice, eaten twice a month, would prevent toothache.

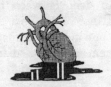

One of the most painfully misguided medical fads of this century was the surgical removal of the colon. Doctors had long been obsessed with the daily evacuation of the bowels, but the king of the colon quacks was Sir William Arbuthnot Lane, a surgeon of Guy's Hospital, London. Earlier in his career Lane, an Irishman and part-time ballroom dancer, recommended oiling the colon daily with a pint of cream and sleeping flat on the belly. He further failed to understand why the medical world was less than impressed with his astonishing discovery that red-haired women were naturally immune to constipation. His greatest contribution to medical science was yet to come: in 1903, he became convinced that the colon was surplus to requirements – it was merely a useless tube of tissue and muscle, full of foul smells and nastiness. With missionary zeal, Lane set about ridding the world of colons. Soon, surgeons all over the country were agreeing with him, and the humble colon took the rap for a whole range of diseases including cancer and tuberculosis. No colon was safe from Lane: patients who came to see him for minor ailments would have their colons removed and tossed into the incinerator as a matter of course. A nagging wife who nearly drove her husband to suicide had her colon whipped out to make her more docile. This ruthless rectal campaign raged for about ten years until fellow doctors, noting that none of Lane's colonless patients ever benefited from their loss, took a more studied look at his theory and began to detect a strong whiff of bullshit. Lane died, discredited, aged 86.

A 1991 Reuter's report from Beijing revealed that a Chinese farmer whose nose was bitten off completely by a huge rat had a brand new, working replacement built from a pig's ear.

Plastic surgery was invented 2000 years ago to save face for Hindu adulterers who, in accordance with the law of the day, were condemned to have their noses ripped off. At first surgeons did their best to cover up the ragged hole by sewing on a lump of skin from the cheek or the forehead. The next great leap forward in plastic surgery took place in 1597 when the Italian Gasparo Tagliacozzi sewed a patient's forearm to his nose; not the most convenient of arrangements as he had to walk around with his arm welded to his face until the transplant took, but it worked. Plastic surgery then took ten steps backward when the Church decided that the operations were the Devil's work: Tagliacozzi's corpse was dug up from his churchyard grave for good measure and reinterred in unconsecrated ground.

Jean Nicot, a French ambassador in Portugal, became famous in 1560 for giving his name to the remarkable new wonder drug nicotine, an antiseptic and universal cure-all which would put an end to ulcers, bites, headaches, colds and rheumatism. A distinguished English doctor hailed Monsieur Nicot's discovery 'one of the best and surest remedies in the world' for apoplexy and giddiness. Tobacco has also been used at various times since to cure asthma, gout, labour pains and even cancer.

Popular nineteenth-century cures for whooping cough included drinking water from the skull of a dead bishop, or sheep droppings boiled in milk. Failing that, you could pass the patient under the belly of a donkey nine times.

Although there are about 650 types of blood-sucking

154

leech, sixteen of them living and breeding happily in Britain, the king of the medicinal variety is *Hirudo medicinalis*, one and a half inches long on an empty stomach, six inches when fully topped up with human blood. In the mid-nineteenth century, France alone had to import 41.5 million of them to satisfy demand. In the 1980s leeches once again became fashionable and were used to clean up clots of blood formed during plastic surgery. In 1987 St Bartholomew's Hospital in London got through 96,000 leeches. If a patient or physician accidentally swallowed one, the recognised cure was a dose of boot blacking in vinegar.

The eighteenth-century English cure for mumps was to lead the patient, in the halter of an ass, three times around a pigsty.

Apart from Admiral Horatio Nelson's terrible fear of seasickness which stayed with him throughout his naval career, he was also an opium addict. His problem dated back to the amputation of his right arm, without anaesthetic, on board the *Theseus* on 25 July 1797. Nelson was so upset by the feel of the cold scalpel against his flesh he ordered that all amputations performed on ships under his command should be done with warm knives. After his arm was cut off he was left to recover with only an opium pill and a shot of rum.

The French Emperor Louis Napoleon III, who suffered from a variety of ailments including dysentery, gonorrhoea and a huge bladder stone, commanded his troops at the Battle of Sedan in 1870 with towels stuffed inside his breeches to act as king-size nappies.

In Sweden in 1994 a man whose hearing was impaired, made a complete recovery after doctors removed a 47-year-old bus ticket from his ear.

Each year about 250 million animals are used by vivisectionists worldwide, and every second of every day an animal dies in an experimental laboratory. The following are some of the actual experiments which have been carried out in the name of medical science on your behalf, and for your benefit: rats submerged in freezing water, or put on hot plates to see how long it takes them to jump; rats plunged in scalding water, and choked with fumes from burning plastic or furniture; live baboons used as crash dummies, and driven into brick walls at 40 mph; cats and rats kept awake for weeks to study how long they will last before they die; rats having their spinal cord severed to see if their sexual reflexes increase; a monkey immobilised in a tank of water with a yoke around its neck, and a breathing tube inserted down its throat to prevent drowning, rocked backwards and forwards until it becomes brain damaged; monkeys placed in 'depression pits' – vertical chambers with smooth, stainless steel sides sloping down towards a base, to see how many days of exhausting and futile activity it takes before they give up on escape and become clinically depressed; squirrel monkeys given electric shocks every twenty seconds until they learn to press a lever: as soon as they learn to do this the lever itself is made live so that it too delivers a shock; fully conscious baboons immersed in scalding water and burned over 50 per cent of their body, then watched for eighteen hours for signs of liver damage; pigs given heart damage by being spun in centrifuges at speeds up to nine times the force of gravity to study the effects of stress on pilots; cats mounted on frames with part of their spinal cord exposed and certain nerves, including those governing genitalia, electrically stimulated; kittens with their eyelids sewn up, having horse-radish peroxide injected into their brains; baby golden hamsters removed from their mothers shortly after birth, having one eye removed, then being returned to their mothers; cats having their eyes wired up to a device which is attached to their skulls with stainless steel screws: the cats are kept awake and their eye movements measured while they are rotated and tilted; rats with different amounts of compressed air being forced into their brains, resulting in brain damage; dozens of pairs of rats sewn together to simulate Siamese twins; condoms pushed into dogs' stomachs and pumped full of water; fully conscious, unanaesthetised cats having mustard injected into their brains; monkeys given drugs to make them develop Parkinson's Disease; monkeys being shot just above the eye to see how long it takes each to die; beagle pups shaved, then their bodies placed in contact with blazing, kerosene-soaked gauze.

Beyond Belief

The biggest, and indeed only tosser in the Bible was Onan, son of Judah, who 'spilled his seed' in the Old Testament (Genesis 38:9). The passage is the basis on which the Church has condemned masturbation for centuries, and gave rise to the word 'onanism', a term for self abuse which was still popular in Victorian times.

The Vatican's Chair of St Peter, the ancient red marble throne on which popes were ceremonially inaugurated, had a hole in the seat, which caused it to resemble an elaborate commode. According to legend, the seat allowed a physical examination of new popes to establish their gender. It was alleged that in the ninth century, the Church had accidentally elected a woman who ruled for two years as Pope John. Her secret was discovered only after she gave birth during a procession.

Hindus have rules which dictate the length of a man's

toothbrush. The correct length for an average Hindu is ten inches. It is shorter for the lower castes, but longer for a Brahmin.

In order to supply the papal choir of the Sistine Chapel with a steady supply of sopranos, the Catholic Church castrated choir boys until 1878.

The feast day of the Christian martyr St Lawrence is 10 August. Legend has it that he was roasted alive on a spit, but faced his death so stoically that he told his torturers, 'Turn me over – I'm cooked on that side.' Today, St Lawrence is the patron saint of rotisseurs.

The US has about 3000 religious cults. Britain has about 600.

A group of villagers in the New Hebrides islands in the Pacific Ocean believe that the Duke of Edinburgh is their messiah, and that he will one day cure all known diseases and grant them eternal youth. Prince Philip's 200 followers expect that on his return he will restore paradise on earth and resume his rightful place among them, wearing the traditional penis gourd. They also believe that Philip secretly runs the Commonwealth and has been able thus far to get away with the tricky business of concealing his true identity from the Queen.

Stream of consciousness

From the Stone Age, mankind the world over was taught that freshwater rivers, springs and water holes were sacred, and that interference with them would bring divine retribution. This wasn't because latter-day priests believed that water was a power greater than mankind itself, but it was a rather effective way of stopping your brethren from shitting in your water supply.

During one particular Syrian religious festival, young men would work themselves into a frenzy, castrate themselves with knives, then run naked through the streets, flinging the amputated private parts into strangers' houses as they went. The house owners were then obliged to provide the young men with clothes.

The 30 August is the feast day of St Fiacre, patron saint of haemorrhoid sufferers.

Because the Koran teaches that pigs are unclean, Miss Piggy used to be edited out of the Muppet Show on Turkish television.

Although the Aztecs are generally considered to have been civilised, they were decadent long before the Spanish arrived on the scene, and their every-day existence was a constant onslaught of barbaric religious brutality. They practised human sacrifice, mostly for reasons of religious ceremony but partly as a means of population control, on an unprecedented scale. The Aztecs butchered and ate well-fed slaves in elaborate ceremonies, and slaughtered captives to provide food for their animals. In one week in 1486, to commemorate the dedication of the temple of Huitzilopichli, about 70,000 captives were marched to the temple in a two-mile long procession and killed. Their elaborate forms of sacrifice, which might include drowning, decapitation, burning or burial alive, were often performed by priests who wore the flayed skins of sacrificed females.

Cardinal sins
Pope John XII turned his papal home the Lateran Palace into a brothel. He and a gang of his friends liked to rape female pilgrims inside the Basilica of St Peter.

Pope Benedict XII was such a hardened boozer that the expression 'drunk as a Pope' become popular in his lifetime.

During the fourteenth-century Holy Inquisition, the church took to digging up the bodies of non-believers it wished to disgrace and publicly mutilating their corpses. The remains of the famous heretic John Wyclif were raised more than 40 years after his death,

161

then burned and tossed in a stream to punish him for his opinions. Sometimes corpses went through mock trials. When Pope Formosus was declared a heretic he was dug up, dressed, condemned by a papal synod then thrown in the Tiber.

Before Joseph Stalin went into politics, he trained to become a priest for five years.

Until the death of Hirohito, Emperors acceding to the Japanese throne had to perform a ritual during which they pretended to have sexual intercourse with the gods.

The Roman Catholic Church adopted celibacy as a code for the priesthood in 1123. Pope Innocent VIII became known as 'The Honest' 350 years later, because he admitted that he had fathered several bastards. He only owned up to disprove a rumour going around Rome at the time that he was a woman.

Until the end of the nineteenth century, parsons were affectionately known as 'bollocks' or 'bollacks'. This little-known fact formed the basis of a successful legal defence in 1978 when the Sex Pistols used it to prevent a nationwide ban on their debut album *Never Mind the Bollocks*.

The feast day of Saints Eulampius and Eulampia, the brother and sister martyrs, is celebrated on 10 November. The couple survived being boiled in oil, moving 200 astonished onlookers to convert to Christianity on the spot. Immediately, all 200 converts were beheaded.

An eighteenth-century German monk named Mayr, who by his close association with Prussia's vacuous King Frederick William II became one of the most powerful men in the country, attempted to demonstrate his deep faith by eating a whole Bible. Mayr lived, although instead of achieving a higher level of consciousness he was only able to achieve a higher level of indigestion. One day Mayr was preaching a sermon from the pulpit when he decided to liven things up by producing two loaded pistols and firing them into the packed congregation. Not a moment too soon, Mayr was certified insane and locked up in an asylum.

In English courtrooms, the custom of kissing a Bible when taking a judicial oath often led to syphilitic infection.

The Catholic Church accepts cannibalism as a justifiable means of saving your own life.

December the 19th is the feast day of Blessed William of Fenoli, a monk who lived in the thirteenth century and who was famous for the odd miracle. According to Christian legend, one day when he was returning from the fields with a mule, he was attacked by robbers. William defended himself by ripping off the leg of his mule, clubbing his attackers with it, then restoring it and continuing on his journey.

Three successive popes, Alexander VI, Julius II and Leo X, all had syphilis.

The early Christians taught that dirtiness was next to Godliness; bathing was an evil, ungodly vanity punishable by an eternity in hell. A fourth-century Christian pilgrim boasted that she hadn't washed her face for eighteen years, and St Francis of Assisi listed personal filthiness among the insignia of piety.

At one time you could be excommunicated from the Catholic Church for wearing a wig.

When anaesthetics first become available in the nineteenth century, the Church opposed the use of them in obstetrics. Childbirth was supposed to hurt, because pain was God's way of punishing women for Eve's sin in the Garden of Eden.

Early Christian teachings encouraged men to castrate themselves to ensure that they would go to Heaven.

Italy's most exclusive cult was founded by an Italian nun, Sister Florence Christina. She left her convent in Bologna in 1989 to reveal to the world that she was receiving God's word on a regular basis via her ten-year-old pet parrot.

The Church in medieval times was faced with a problem whenever a pregnant woman died, as unbaptised babies were not allowed burial in Christian cemeteries. The foetus would often be cut from the mother's corpse and buried outside the cemetery in unconsecrated ground.

Many early Christian monks and nuns believed that the body fluids of the deceased, especially those of saints or clergymen, had special medicinal and curative properties. Among the effluvia of a corpse that would be used to make tinctures, oils and balms were blood, saliva, ear wax, urine, faeces and sperm.

All Things Bright and Beautiful

Thanks to a high-fibre diet of bamboo which keeps it chewing for up to fourteen hours non-stop, the giant panda has to defecate about 48 times a day.

Nature's most ruthless rapist is a parasitic wasp whose natural habitat is the inside of green vegetables. As soon as the tiny parasite is born, he waits beside the female eggs of his sisters so that he can rape them incestuously the moment they are hatched.

The ladybird is the only insect known to suffer from a sexually transmitted venereal disease. The infection manifests itself as a highly unpleasant form of lice which is passed on during the ladybird's three-hour orgies.

Before bears go into hibernation they plug up their anus with bits of wood, stones, pine leaves or anything else that comes to hand. They do this to stop ants from crawling into their bowels while they are asleep.

Every day, dogs dump 1000 tons of faeces and spray 990,000 gallons of urine onto the streets, parks, footpaths and public places in Britain – equivalent to the output of ten million humans.

A bed-tick bloated with human blood can swell to the size of a golf-ball.

An Alsatian guide dog for the blind was described by his trainer as 'basically a damn good guide dog' after accidentally killing its fourth owner in 1993. 'Lucky' led the first one under a car, the second under a bus, the third in front of a train, and the fourth over a pier. The authorities decided to give him another chance: intriguingly, they also decided not to inform the new owner about Lucky's previous form.

The pleasant-tasting death cap mushroom *Amanita phalloides* can be easily mistaken for the edible variety, but is one of the most lethal plant poisons known to man. The toxin works by dissolving human blood corpuscles. The symptoms do not appear until nine to fourteen hours later. Less than a third of the people who have ever eaten it lived.

On average about 2000 spiders lurk inside every British house.

The noctuid moth, native to Malaysia and Thailand, has a penchant for human eyes. It likes to fly into people's faces and feed on optical discharge, causing the eye to become severely inflamed.

The male water mite is one of nature's premier sado-masochists. The mite, whose legs double as sex organs, ties down his partner with tiny hooks and then even glues himself to her body to make sure she doesn't escape while he rapes her.

Two-thirds of all dog faeces are infected with a great number of potentially harmful diseases, the worst of which is toxocariasis, a disease carried in roundworm eggs, which can cause blindness, asthma, epilepsy or even death, depending on where the eggs migrate within the system. The eggs can survive in soil for up to three years and cannot be destroyed with disinfectant or freezing temperatures. Over 300 cases of infection, mostly in children, are treated in Britain every year, but this is probably a tiny proportion of the underlying problem: it is estimated that 16,000 new infestations occur every year.

Rats have to gnaw with their chisel-shaped upper incisors all day long. If they didn't, their teeth would grow at a rate of four inches a year and would curl around and up through the palate, cutting into the brain.

Owing to an administrative error by mother nature, the female bedbug is born without a sex organ. The male bedbug has a pointed penis, with which he drills a hole in his partner's gut and deposits his sperm in her bloodstream.

A peckish leech can consume two fluid ounces of human blood in ten minutes.

Two of nature's most antisocial defence mechanisms are employed by seabirds: the fieldfar and the fulmar. The former discourages marauding predators with an aerial bombardment of excrement: it can target with pinpoint accuracy, the smell is repulsive, and is able to mount wave after wave of attack. Fulmars protect their cliffside nests by projectile vomiting: the seabird's pungent-smelling puke can hit an intruder 3–4 feet away.

The single greatest concentration of rats in the UK is believed to be beneath the Houses of Parliament.

A puncture wound from the dorsal fin of a stonefish will cause paralysis of the limbs, respiratory failure, convulsions and finally death, usually within six hours.

Starfish are capable of turning their stomachs inside out.

A distressed octopus will sometimes commit suicide by eating itself.

The female earwig rears nature's most ungrateful offspring. The selfless mother rarely leaves her young until they are capable of looking after themselves, and often starves herself in the process. This maternal devotion is poorly repaid by the growing nymphs, who quickly eat her as soon as she falls ill and dies.

Calyptra eustigata, the world's only blood-sucking moth, can penetrate even the hide of a rhinoceros or elephant.

Rats carry dozens of different diseases which can kill or seriously harm human beings, including bubonic plague, Lassa fever, encephalitis, three species of salmonella, typhus, liver worm, Chaga's disease, toxoplasmosis, trichinosis, pneumocytis carinii, yersiniosis, erysipelis and several fungal diseases. They are also the sole carrier of Weil's disease, which is distributed in rat urine and causes several deaths in Britain every year.

A hungry ribbon worm can eat up to 95 per cent of its own body weight, and live.

The mechanics by which the charmless flea *Xenopsylla cheopsis* transfers bubonic plague from the black rat to humans are almost as gruesome as the plague symptoms. The plague bacillus is carried in the rat's blood, where it rapidly multiplies. The flea feeds on the rat's blood, and the bacteria then divides and forms a solid mass inside the flea's stomach. The flea becomes 'blocked' and suffers acute hunger. When it tries again to feed on a warm-blooded human, the flea's gullet is stretched to the limit and infected blood is regurgitated back into the open wound. When a flea feeds it automatically defecates, depositing bacteria in its faeces. The victim, irritated by the flea bite, scratches the wound and fatally spreads the bacteria-infested flea faeces.

In the first 48 hours of its life the larva of the North American polyphemus moth eats the equivalent of 86,000 times its own body weight.

When the female bedbug can't find any human blood on which to feed, she will happily dine on her male partner's semen.

The world's biggest known germ, *Epulopiscium*, lives in the intestines of surgeonfish, mice and guinea pigs. It is a million times bigger than any germ, and is the only form of bacteria large enough to be seen by the naked eye.

The female black widow spider can eat up to 25 mates in one day.

Cockroaches and rats are probably two of the only creatures who would survive a nuclear holocaust. Cockroaches are resistant to radiation, can exist without food or water for a month, and a single mating pair can produce 400,000 offspring in one year. Rats will live quite happily for years on stuff that human beings avoid stepping in, and a pair of breeding rats can produce 15,000 offspring in one year. The Ministry of Agriculture acknowledges the existence of a new breed of British 'super rat', which breeds at an even more phenomenal rate than the ordinary rat and is resistant to conventional rat poisons such as Warfarin.

The malaria parasite, which kills more than one million babies and children every year, has been responsible for about 50 per cent of all human deaths since the Stone Age.

The black woodpecker of North America, which hammers wood at the rate of 15–16 times per second at a top speed of 1300 miles per hour, has to hit the target with its beak, head and neck in an absolutely straight line, every time: if it didn't, the force would tear its brains out.

When mountain gorillas fancy a hot meal on a cold day instead of the usual boring salad, they eat their own faeces.

Private Members

The eighteenth-century Tory Party leader Viscount Bolingbroke was as well known for his debauchery as his oratory. He once described a perfect day: 'Got drunk, harangued the Queen, and at night was put to bed by a beautiful lady, and was tuck'd up by two of the prettiest young Peers in England, Lords Jersey and Bathurst.'

The radical MP John Wilkes was a famous bisexual. The Earl of Sandwich once remarked to him, 'I don't know whether you'll die on the gallows or of the pox.' 'That depends,' replied Wilkes, 'whether I first embrace your Lordship's principles or your Lordship's mistress.'

Britain's seventh Prime Minister, the Earl of Bute (1762–3), was variously alleged to have had an adulterous affair with the Prince of Wales's wife Augusta and a homosexual relationship with her son the young King George III.

The Earl of Chatham (Prime Minister 1766–8), had a family history of mental illness. He had several mental breakdowns and his appearances in the House of Commons became increasingly rare and eccentric. Eventually he became a total recluse and spent all his time locked in his bedroom while food was passed to him through a hatch.

The Earl of Grafton (Prime Minister 1768–70), wasn't the first adulterous PM, but he was the first to flaunt his mistress in front of the reigning monarch, and the first known to have slept with his mistress at 10 Downing Street. Her name was Nancy Parsons.

Henry Addington (Prime Minister 1801–4) didn't dare face the Commons until he was drunk, and would prepare for his speeches by downing about five bottles of wine.

William Pitt the Younger (Prime Minister 1783–1801 and 1804–6) was advised as a young man to drink a bottle of port a day for his health. He took it to heart: at his peak he would daily consume six bottles of port, two bottles of Madeira and one and a half bottles of claret. He drank himself to death aged 46.

Britain's nineteenth-century Foreign Minister Lord Castlereagh had a complete mental breakdown halfway through the peace settlement at the end of the

Napoleonic Wars. In 1822, the Bishop of Clogher, a member of the House of Lords, was caught in a London tavern buggering a young soldier. Castlereagh became obsessed with the idea that he too might be charged with homosexual offences and killed himself by slashing his own throat with a penknife.

George Canning (Prime Minister 1827) was a laudanum addict and almost certainly had an affair with the then Prince Regent's wife, the none too fragrant Caroline of Brunswick.

The famous retort by the Duke of Wellington (Prime Minister 1827–8), 'Publish and be damned!' was his response to the blackmailer Joseph Stockdale, who threatened to print the memoirs of Wellington's favourite prostitute, Harriette Wilson. Stockdale did publish, and so the whole of London was able to read about the Iron Duke's prowess between the sheets, which, according to the high class tart, was 'most unentertaining' and 'very uphill work'. Wellington's stance wasn't quite as brave as it was often painted: he threatened to sue for libel, but the writ never materialised.

Queen Victoria's first Prime Minister Lord Melbourne (1835–41) was a sexual pervert, addicted to flagellation.

He was a heavy drinker, and was in a drunken stupor throughout Victoria's coronation. His excuse was that he was suffering from violent constipation, and had to get through the ceremony by swigging large quantities of brandy and laudanum. He didn't attend Cabinet meetings after that for a week.

Viscount Palmerston (Prime Minister 1855–8 and 1859–65) was an habitual womaniser who was cited as co-respondent in a divorce case at the age of 79. Only the Duke of Wellington could better this: he started an affair when he was 83.

Palmerston tried to rape one of Queen Victoria's ladies-in-waiting while he was visiting Windsor Castle. He defended his behaviour by claiming he was blind drunk on port and had entered the wrong bedroom. The whole matter was hushed up, but Victoria never believed his story, nor did she forgive him.

The Tory Cabinet Minister Lewis 'Loulou' Harcourt was described as a bisexual 'sex maniac'. He killed himself after being accused of the attempted rape of a young girl; he also attempted to assault the girl's brother sexually. *The Complete Peerage* wrote up the cause of his death as a heart attack in his sleep.

The Liberal Prime Minister William Gladstone spent his evenings prowling London's brothels 'rescuing' prostitutes, afterwards flogging himself with a whip. He admitted he was a pushover for a pretty face.

The late nineteenth-century Liberal Cabinet Minister, Sir Charles 'Three-in-a-bed' Dilke, resigned after being named as co-respondent in a divorce case. During the trial it was revealed that he had slept with the young wife of a fellow MP and persuaded her to allow his maid to join them, teaching the MP's wife 'every French vice'.

One of the top Tories of his day, the Marquess of Hartington, known as 'Harty-Tarty', shared London's best known high-class prostitute Catherine 'Skittles' with, among others, King Edward VII. Hartington kept her on £2000 a year and bought her a house in Mayfair.

Yes, Minister, Yes . . .

Herbert Henry Asquith (Prime Minister 1908–16) admitted to 'a slight weakness for the companionship of clever and attractive women'. This was a slight understatement, as he was a regular and habitual womaniser, who at the age of 62 had an affair with the 27-year-old friend of his daughter. He was also a heavy drinker and once appeared on the front bench during an important debate too pissed to speak.

In 1917, the right wing MP Pemberton Billing was accused of libelling a well-known dancer by calling her a lesbian. During his trial, he claimed to have assembled a list of 47,000 perverts, adulterers, nymphomaniacs, drunks and homosexuals in high places. He was acquitted, and wildly applauded both

in court and by thousands outside. It was believed that
the Judge and Asquith were both on his list.

Never had it so good. . .

Lloyd George (Prime Minister 1916–22) lived a scan-
dalous double life, spending half his time with his wife
and the other half in the bed of his secretary, Frances
Stevenson. The press turned a blind eye to the affair,
even when he fathered an illegitimate daughter. He
also slept with his daughter's governess, who was
about half his age. When his son answered a phone
call enquiring if the mistress of the house was available, he replied 'Which mistress?'

Lloyd George charged £10,000 for a knighthood,
£30,000 for a baronetcy, and up to £100,000 for a
peerage.

The first Labour Prime Minister, Ramsay MacDonald
(1924, 1929–35), was accused of being a class traitor
when he had an affair with leading Tory 'hostess' the
Marchioness of Londonderry.

Ramsay MacDonald began to lose his mind while he

was in office. He suffered from what he called 'brain-fag' – probably the slow onset of premature senile dementia. As he deteriorated his speeches became more and more incomprehensible, and towards the end of his career he dreaded appearing at the dispatch box because even he hadn't a clue what he was supposed to be talking about. At a disarmament conference in Geneva he again lost the thread of his speech and told his puzzled audience: 'Be men, not mannequins.'

Sir Winston Churchill was a major piss artist, but at least he was quite open about his problem. He once tried to persuade Saudi Arabia's strict Moslem King Ibn Saud that he drank alcohol because it was part of his religion. Although it wrecked his health and he suffered several minor strokes, he claimed, 'I have taken more out of alcohol than alcohol has taken out of me.'

Harold Macmillan's term in office (1957–63) was bedevilled by a series of sex scandals including the Profumo affair, at a time when his own wife was supposed to be having a liaison with one of his Tory Cabinet Ministers. One day John F. Kennedy turned to Macmillan and said, 'If I don't get a woman for three days, I get a terrible headache . . . how is it with you Harold?'

In 1958, Macmillan's junior Foreign Office Minister Ian Harvey resigned after he was caught behaving in a manner 'likely to offend against public decency with a nineteen-year-old Guardsman under a tree in St James's Park, London'. On the way to the police station the MP gave a false name and tried to run off.

Another prominent member of Macmillan's Government, Sir Ian Horobin, used to sexually assault young boys after inviting them to see his stamp collection. He admitted ten charges of indecency with young men and boys at the Old Bailey in 1962.

The homosexual Labour MP Tom Driberg, (or 'William Hickey' to *Daily Express* readers) admitted a liking for 'rough trade'. When he joined the House of Commons he was given a formal tour of the 'most important rooms' in the Palace of Westminister by the Tory MP Henry Channon: they turned out to be the men's toilets. Driberg, who was also on MI5's payroll, admitted he used his status as a British spy to get him off the hook every time the police caught him importuning young men in public lavatories.

Lord Lambton, a Parliamentary Under-Secretary in Edward Heath's Tory Government, resigned after admitting taking drugs, including opium and regularly visiting prostitutes while married. He said later, 'I can't think what all the fuss is about. Surely all men patronise whores.'

Back to basics

Former Liberal Party leader Jeremy Thorpe stood trial for conspiring to murder his gay lover Norman Scott. It was his evidence that gave the English language the phrase 'pillow biter'.

Margaret Thatcher's Sex Appeal, and Worse . . .

In 1993, a Japanese opinion poll voted Margaret Thatcher the World's Sexiest Woman, ahead of Brooke Shields, Michelle Pfeiffer and Sharon Stone.

Austria's Empress Maria Theresa was a notoriously hard woman who had sixteen children. She was working on her government papers when she went into labour with her fifteenth child, Marie Antoinette; the Empress took the opportunity to call for her dentist and have a bad tooth pulled, as she figured she wouldn't notice the extra pain. As soon as the baby was delivered she went straight back to her paperwork.

The first ever Caesarean birth, recorded in 1500, was carried out by a pig gelder.

In 1603 in London alone, 30,000 of Queen Elizabeth's subjects died of the plague. 'Good Queen Bess' responded to the national crisis by fleeing with her court to Windsor Castle, where she had a gallows set up and promised to hang anyone who tried to follow her.

Florence Nightingale was a noted hypochondriac who steadfastly refused to believe in the existence of bacteria even as it wiped out half of her patients.

The Russian Empress Anne loved hunting, but couldn't be bothered with the thrill of a long chase, or for that matter of any chase at all; most of the time she didn't even get out of her carriage. A special hunting area was prepared in the park at Peterhof which was so thick with imported bears, wild boars, stags and other animals that all she had to do was poke her gun out of her carriage window to be sure of hitting something. Yet nothing was left to chance: to ensure that she went home with plenty of trophies, the animals were driven past the muzzle of her gun at point-blank range. Every now and then the Empress would indulge in a bit of hunting without even getting out of bed. On these occasions, the palace aviary was always fully stocked so she could have a few flocks to shoot at from her bedroom window.

It takes more water to make one rubber car tyre than it does to keep a thirsty child alive for six months.

Lesbianism was rife amongst the damsels who lounged in the harems of the Ottoman Sultans. Although the watchful eunuchs were expected to put a stop to it, they were unable to stamp it out completely. A

Venetian envoy noted that the harem girls were particularly fond of cucumbers but that 'they are sent in unto them sliced, to deprive them of the meanes of playing the wantons.'

After Queen Victoria inhaled chloroform to help her through the birth of her seventh child, Anaesthesia briefly became a fashionable christian name for baby girls.

In France, there used to be a Midsummer's Day tradition of tossing live cats onto a public bonfire to listen to them scream. The French also tortured cats at fairgrounds for general public amusement.

One of the stolen gems which now forms part of the British Crown Jewels is the Koh-i-noor diamond, seized from India after the defeat of the Maharajah of the Punjab at Lahore, and presented to Queen Victoria in 1851. The huge diamond, regarded as India's most fabulous treasure, was the largest in the world at that time. In 1854, when the Maharajah visited Buckingham Palace, Queen Victoria demonstrated breathtaking tactlessness when she casually showed it off to its rightful owner. The Maharajah reacted with dignity to the massive insult, but thereafter always referred to Queen Victoria as 'Mrs Fagin'. India still regards the diamond as its national treasure, and to this day considers that Queen Elizabeth II is in receipt of stolen property.

In western Australia in the nineteenth century, Aboriginals controlled the size of their tribe by eating every tenth baby born.

In 1623, the Profane Oaths Act made swearing illegal in England. The popular oaths of the day, the colourful 'Gog's malt', the suggestive 'Cat's nouns', or the extremely naughty 'a turd i' your teeth' could earn you a shilling fine or a good whipping. Most people took no notice and carried on swearing, and so in 1745 the law was beefed up with stiffer penalties. By this time most people were saying 'stap me vitals' or possibly even 'ods niggers noggers' to the Act, which curiously enough lay neglected on the statute books for over 200 years until it was repealed in 1967.

To meet the rules of breed standards for show purposes, many pedigree dogs are bred to the point of deformity. Pekinese bitches are often incapable of whelping properly and have to be delivered by Caesarean section. They also often suffer from cleft palates and chronic breathing and eyesight problems. Cavalier King Charles spaniels suffer from disc and heart problems, and West Highland whites are prone to eye and skin disease. Many Dalmatians are also born deaf as a result of inbreeding, and many breeds have deformed kneecaps. Large breeds like Dobermanns,

185

Labradors and Great Danes often suffer from spinal deformity.

When Prince Albert unveiled his plan for a crystal palace, experts confidently predicted that the London sparrows who perched on it would crush the whole structure with the combined weight of their droppings.

The word 'rooster' was invented to describe male chickens because Americans were too embarrassed to contemplate using the word 'cock'.

The bane of nineteenth-century bodysnatchers' lives was the distinctive aroma which told them that the corpse they'd just struggled to dig up was more than eight to ten days old, and therefore far too decomposed to be of any use to a medical student. All was not completely lost, however, because the more enterprising 'resurrection men' knew all about asset stripping. They could find customers for the brass coffin fittings, sell the coffin for firewood, the bones for manure, the teeth to the toothless, and melt the body down and sell the fat to candlemakers.

In 1943 a unit of Gurkha soldiers fighting in the British Army in Burma made a series of commando raids along the coast of Japanese-held Arakan. When they returned claiming to have killed over one hundred of the enemy, the Gurkhas were understandably miffed when British officers treated their story with undisguised scepticism. They made sure no one doubted their word when they returned from the next raid loaded down with sacks full of Japanese heads.

In Ancient Rome, men traditionally took an oath by grabbing their testicles with the right hand.

I know a dead tortoise when I see one . . .
The highest amount ever paid for a deceased tortoise was the £49 forked out by a Mrs D. Cobb in 1992. When she became suspicious about her pet's apparent inactivity, a sales representative from the Reptile Kingdom, Luton, explained to her that it was 'probably shy'.

The severed heads of dead pets are often sold as animal feed to zoos and safari parks.

Factory-reared chickens often have to have their beaks removed to stop them from attacking, or even eating each other. Mechanical 'debeaking machines' use hot blades to cut through a highly sensitive area of tissue around the chicken's mouth. In some parts of the US, the beaks are burned off.

The Nirhor tribe in India were endo-cannibals, i.e. people who only ate friends and relatives; the very thought of eating a stranger made them nauseous. Whenever a Nirhor tribesman fell ill, his closest friends would kill and eat him before his meat was spoiled by disease. Even if the victim protested that he might be getting better, they would kill and eat him anyway. It was a no-win situation: any Nirhor tribesman lucky enough to reach a great age would be sacrificed and eaten by way of celebration.

The English writer William Hazlitt gave an eye-witness account of many of the worst atrocities of the French Revolution. At Bordeaux, a woman who wept because her husband was about to be guillotined was forced to sit beneath the blade while his blood dripped onto her, then she too was executed. When King Louis XVI went to the guillotine on 21 January 1793, hundreds of men and women rioted while trying to dip their fingers in the royal blood.

When Rumanian President Nicolae Ceauçescu and his wife Elena were summarily executed by a firing squad on Christmas Day 1989, the soldiers fired so enthusiastically that they even shot each other.

The Greek Commander General Hajianestis, who led his country's army in the war with Turkey in 1921, was believed at the time to have been completely insane, but in fact showed a keen sense of self preservation. Rather than rouse himself to command his troops, he lay in bed pretending to be dead. Another ploy he sometimes used was to claim that he couldn't get up because his legs were made of glass and they might break if he moved.

Before his electrocution in New Jersey, murderer Charles Fithina told his wardens, 'I want to make a complaint ... the soup I had for supper tonight was too hot.'

A 1911 mail-order offer in the US netted hundreds of thousands of dollars with the promise of a miracle cure that could turn blacks into whites. The most outrageous American mail-order con of all time, however, began in 1946 and lasted for a decade. William Johnson, a semi-literate miner from Kentucky, decided to cash in on a rumour sweeping America that Adolf Hitler had been smuggled out of Europe after World War II and was alive and well and living in North America. Johnson posed as the Führer, who had now supposedly settled in Kentucky with some of his Nazi chiefs of staff and was planning to take over the US. He made a public appeal for cash to help his cause, and right wing Americans and fascists of German extraction sent him a steady stream of postal orders as he elaborated his dastardly plans for space ships, 'invisible ships' and underground hoards of ammunition. The fact that he often signed his name as 'The Furrier' didn't stop the American public from sending him tens of thousands of dollars.

The current in-vogue import in Japan is deformed animals from the Chernobyl region. The craze began in 1992 when a stuffed two-headed calf appeared outside a restaurant in Kyoto. An estimated 70 per cent of the calves born around the site of the Soviet nuclear accident are deformed.

A craze for swallowing live goldfish began at Harvard College, Boston in 1939, after a student named Lothrop Withington Junior did it to win a $10 bet. Two of his friends told the college newspaper, and soon the main Boston newspapers were reporting it. Suddenly goldfish swallowing became fashionable, and throughout the spring of 1939 the US goldfish population nosedived as students all over the country vied to outdo each other in the consumption of finny comestibles. An unofficial record for goldfish swallowing was established – 43 in one sitting – although the teenager who accomplished this was kicked out of his school for 'conduct unbecoming a student'.

On average every glass of London tap water has already passed through the bladders of nine other people.

After victimising everyone else he could think of, Mao Tse-tung mobilised the entire Chinese nation to take it out on the birds. Sparrows are notorious for eating cereal crops, and so over a period of 48 hours, about 80 million Chinese took to the streets and fields and banged woks and gongs until the birds dropped dead of exhaustion. It was a popular move with most people because the Chinese loved fried sparrow. Without the sparrows to control worms and other pests, however, agricultural disaster followed. With the alteration in the natural food cycle, 43 million people starved to death over the next three years.

In Thailand, elephants are fed amphetamines to make them work longer.

In the 1920s at least 31 American states had laws which legally allowed them to sterilise people whom they classified as 'defectives', in an attempt to purify the genetic composition of their population. In 1927, the US Supreme Court upheld eugenic sterilisation laws on the grounds that the offspring of people of limited intelligence, the mentally ill and members of what they defined as the 'criminal classes' had no right to exist because they would be an unfair burden on decent, law-abiding, tax-paying Americans. Although the stigma of the obvious Nazi connotation led some US states to repeal their laws after World War II, 21 of them retained their sterilisation laws until as late as the 1980s.

Apart from Saudi Arabians, Britons are the only people in the world denied a written constitution by their state.

By law, a copy of every new book published has to be deposited with the British Library, irrespective of subject matter. Their catalogue lists the following titles: *The Romance of Leprosy*, E. Mackerchar, 1949; *Why*

Bring That Up? A Guide to Seasickness; J. F. Montague, 1936; *Penetrating Wagner's Ring*, John L. Di Gaetanao, 1978; *Scouts in Bondage*, Geoffrey Prout, 1930; *Jews at a Glance*, Mac Davis, 1956; *Constipation and Our Civilization*, J. C. Thomson, 1943; *A Pictorial Book of Tongue Coating*, Anon., 1981; *A Government Committee of Enquiry on the Light Metal Artificial Leg*, Captain Henry Hulme Chisholm Baird, 1923; *Daddy Was An Undertaker*, McDill, McGown and Gassman, 1952; *A Short Account of the Origin, Progress and Present State of the New Rupture Society*, Anon., 1816; *Teach Yourself Alcoholism*, Meier Glatt, 1975; *How to Cook Husbands*, Elizabeth Strong Worthington, 1899; *A Study of Masturbation and its Reputed Sequelae*, J. F. W. Meagher, 1924; and *Sex After Death*, B. J. Ferrell & D. E. Frey, 1983.

In France, menstruation is known as *avoir les anglais* – 'to have the Englishes'.

Bullfighting in Spain would probably have been banned years ago if it weren't for the entertainment of foreign and, more often than not, British tourists. Opinion polls show that about 93 per cent of the population of Spain either no longer support bullfighting, or abhor it and want to see it abolished. In the last 225 years in which figures have been available for bullfights taking place in Spain and South America, 58 matadors and mounted bullfighters have died. During this same period 1.3 million bulls have been cruelly put to death, and over 40,000 horses have been either

192

crushed to death or disembowelled in Spain alone. The bull is usually unwilling to fight, and has to be either goaded into action with stimulants, or injected with sedatives if it becomes too frisky. There are a variety of traditional tricks to make sure that the bull doesn't pose a genuine threat to the matador, including plugging one nostril with cotton wool to interfere with the bull's breathing and make sure it tires quickly, pouring laudanum into its ears, and sticking a darning needle through its testicles.

About 30,000 foxes die every year as a result of organised blood sports.

Art for art's sake

An art exhibition in Scarborough in 1992 featured a dismembered dog chopped into nine pieces and suspended from the ceiling, 63 squashed mice mounted in plastic, and the butchered remains of three rabbits. The artist, Catherine Gregory, said she did it for the animal rights movement.

In 1971, an American artist Newton Harrison staged an art exhibition at the Hayward Gallery, London called 'Portable Fish Farm' at which he planned to publicly electrocute 60 live catfish. The electrocution was finally called off after a protest by Spike Milligan, who made his feelings known by lobbing a brick through the Hayward Gallery window.

A New York cable TV channel once filmed a small dog being tied to a stake and shot with a rifle. The 30-second sequence was repeated for 30 minutes and presented as a conceptual art piece, titled *Shot Dog Film*. The film was partially funded with a grant from the US National Endowment for the Arts, a government agency which gives US tax money to cultural projects.

Slaves sent into the Roman amphitheatres to fight wild animals often had their teeth removed and their arms broken to ensure that they didn't damage the Emperor's valuable livestock.

US Government officials gave the opening of their brand new Department of Agriculture staff canteen a glorious send-off in 1977, when they staged an official opening ceremony attended by the Agriculture Secretary. Robert Bergland duly unveiled a brass plaque naming it the 'Alfred Packer Memorial Dining Facility', after one of America's most famous nineteenth-century frontiersmen. A few months later the plaque was hurriedly removed when someone remembered what the late Mr Packer had been chiefly famous for: he was a cannibal, convicted of killing and eating five Colorado gold prospectors in the 1870s.

Exit

In Athens in ancient times, the local magistrate would keep a supply of poison handy for any elderly, depressed or terminally ill person who wanted to commit suicide: all you had to do was ask permission to drink it.

In nineteenth-century Britain, failed suicides were hanged.

In some Inuit cultures, if an elderly or infirm person tells his family he is ready to die, they will oblige by either killing him on the spot or abandoning him in the cold and letting nature take its course.

The ancient Britons practised euthanasia by throwing themselves off overhanging rocks: if they were too old to jump, someone would give them a shove.

About 1000 people commit suicide every day.

Scandinavians practised euthanasia by putting their old people in big earthenware jars and leaving them to die.

Hungary has the world's highest suicide rate.

Old Ethiopians who wanted to die allowed themselves to be tied to wild bulls.

Congolese natives used to jump up and down on their elderly or terminally ill relatives until they had finished them off.

More American veterans of the Vietnam war have died by suicide since their return than were actually killed in battle.

The Hottentot tribe of Africa used to give their senior citizens a huge farewell party before abandoning them to die in a hut in the wilderness.

In Ceos, in Ancient Greece, it was obligatory for people over the age of sixty to commit suicide.

Zeno was the Greek responsible for Stoicism, a school of philosophy whose devotees maintain an impassive attitude to both pleasure or pain. He hanged himself at the age of 98 after falling down and wrenching his finger.

URBAN MYTHS
Phil Healey and Rick Glanvill

This hilarious collection of contemporary 'true stories' unleashes over 200 new, borrowed and blue urban myths, starring the ubiquitous 'friend-of-a-friend'. They're saucy, implausible, bizarre and sometimes scary – and as with all the best yarns, they have a spooky ring of truth. In a society obsessed by gossip, URBAN MYTHS are the best unfounded stories around. Read them here and never trust that, 'No, but it really happened' line again.

ISBN 0 86369 686 4

THE RETURN OF URBAN MYTHS
Phil Healey and Rick Glanvill

More incredible but 'true' stories of sex, drink and unreliable machinery – featuring the live Xmas turkey, the Mexican tobacco pouch, and over 200 other astounding 'friend of a friend' classics. A glowing testament to the sordid inventiveness of the human mind, this new literary twist on an age-old form plumbs the depths of society's irrational prejudices, unquenchable gullibility and sheer stupidity. Spice up any conversation with this fresh and fruity cocktail of comical cautionary tales.

ISBN 0 86369 752 6

URBAN MYTHS – UNPLUGGED
Phil Healey and Rick Glanvill

They said it could never be done, but here it is ... the third, acoustic version of the best-selling URBAN MYTHS series. You split your sides with the first, bust a blood vessel over the second, so go ahead, snap a gusset with UNPLUGGED. Once again, Messrs Healey and Glanvill pay tribute to the fiendish storytelling genius of humankind, gathering together mad, bad and dangerous examples of downright daftness. All human life is here, and quite a few animals too.

ISBN 0 86369 897 2